The Problem Horse

AN OWNER'S GUIDE

KAREN BUSH

The Crowood Press

First published in 1992 by
The Crowood Press Ltd
Ramsbury, Marlborough
Wiltshire SN8 2HR

Paperback edition 1995

© Karen Bush 1992

British Library Cataloguing in Publication Data

A catalogue record for this book is available from the British Library

ISBN 1 85223 916 6

Dedication
For Mick

Picture Credits
Black and white photographs by the author
Line-drawings by Hazel Morgan

Throughout this book, he, his and him have been used as
neutral pronouns and are intended to refer to both sexes.

Typeset by Taurus Graphics, Abingdon, Oxon.
Printed in Great Britain by
Butler & Tanner Ltd, Frome.

Contents

Acknowledgements

I should firstly like to thank Bob and Kay DeLuca, and the staff and clients (both human and equine) of Bramley Farm, Little Kingshill, Buckinghamshire, for agreeing to pose so patiently for the many photographs reproduced here, and also those members of the general public who may have unwittingly found themselves and their horses captured on film for posterity!

Grateful thanks are due to Charles Harris FABRS, FIH, FBHS, for kindly allowing me to quote him several times in both the introduction and the first chapter – and also for all the encouragement and support he has offered over the years, not only just to myself personally, but to all those interested in matters equine.

Thanks also to Mike Wood for taking many of the photographs, and to Martello Plastics for permission to reproduce the photograph of the rider using one of their plastic mounting blocks on page 113.

Last, but certainly not least, I am indebted to Mike Fleming for kindly photocopying the manuscript for me!

Introduction

Think, treat your horse as your friend and your rewards will be much greater than treating him as your slave . . .

(Charles Harris)

The modern horse is the product of millions of years of specialized evolution; their bodies and social behaviour have adapted over the years not to meet our own needs, but to enable them to survive in sometimes hostile surroundings. Unfortunately, this fact is all too often overlooked, and as we subject our equine friends to ever greater physical stresses whilst keeping them in increasingly artificial environments, it is no wonder that we encounter 'problems' with them. What is most convenient and desirable for us is not always in the best interests of the horse.

In order to deal effectively with such difficulties as may occur – or better still to avoid them in the first place – it is essential for the horse owner to have an appreciation of how the horse functions, both physically and psychologically.

These two aspects are closely related, physical well-being having an effect on behaviour and vice versa. This can easily be related to yourself: if you are troubled by something, it is unlikely that your own work will be particularly impressive. Similarly, if you are feeling unwell, it is much more difficult to concentrate and you are quite likely to be irritable as well. The difference between horses and

humans is that the latter have a higher degree of intelligence and imagination, and possess greater powers of reasoning, which means that when we feel a bit below par or are depressed, we are able to keep going with whatever task is in hand. Where the horse is concerned, he cannot understand why he should!

As an amateur or professional owner, or as someone who simply enjoys spending a little spare time in the company of horses, your enjoyment of them can only be increased by applying a little thought, logic and common sense to your activities with them. Some time should also be set aside for simply observing them in their environment, and especially noting any changes in behaviour as well as performance, for this can often provide valuable clues to the underlying causes of any problems which do crop up. The genuine horse lover and enthusiast will not find this too unpleasant a task, and the rewards that can be reaped by learning how to 'tune in' to individual horses will far outweigh any expense in terms of time.

It is hoped that this book will help you to understand the horses you come into contact with a little better, and in the case of those that have what could be described as a problem of some kind, better equip you to search out the cause as well as the remedy for yourself. Various causes and remedies are suggested for those problems that are most commonly encountered, but it is always worth bearing in mind the old maxim that 'many roads lead to Rome'. You may find that one particular approach works better for your horse than another; you may even go on to devise your own particular solution based on your observations and which is equally as safe, effective and, in the long term, satisfactory.

No one person, or book, can pretend to possess all the answers, especially since all horses are individuals and each problem needs to be dealt with keeping this in mind. It is probably true to say that the most important requirement of anyone dealing with horses is the ability to keep an open mind and to be prepared to be flexible and adaptable. In this respect I can do no better than to quote Charles Harris once again:

. . . *a keen rider [or horse manager] should observe, reflect and experiment – observation collates the facts, reflection brings them together, and experiment confirms the results* . . .

CHAPTER 1

Know your Horse

The Horse and Evolution

The horse first appeared on Earth about 55 million years ago, although in a somewhat different form to that of the animal we are familiar with today. Its distant ancestor Eohippus was a four-toed, fox-sized creature with short hair, a thick neck, eyes set to the front of its head and a stumpy tail.

It lived by browsing on shrubs rather than grazing, but as the climate changed and forests and grassland replaced jungles and swamps, Eohippus had to adapt and evolve to meet the challenges posed by the new physical conditions. The limbs became longer and simplified, enabling the horse to run faster and escape from predators. The result is that the modern equine now stands virtually on the tips of his toes. The neck became longer to facilitate grazing and at the same time the head became longer so that the eyes were above grass level, and positioned to the sides to give better all-round vision of any potential predators. Funnel-shaped ears developed for improved hearing; the body shape altered to allow extra heart and

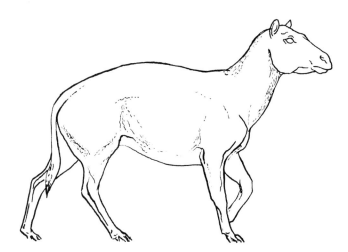

Fig 1 The distant ancestor of the modern horse was better adapted to living in wooded, swampy areas. Changes in environment brought about considerable differences in his appearance to enable him to survive.

lung space to assist in flight; and a large abdomen overcame the problems posed by a large intake of hard-to-digest plant matter.

It is generally accepted that the horse was first domesticated by Man between 5,000 and 6,000 years ago. On the whole he has adapted very well, but nevertheless we still ask a great deal of him. He has, after all, spent millions of years evolving into a specialized form never intended to be used for the purposes to which we have put him; on the overall time scale, he has been our servant for only a relatively short period. It is not surprising to discover, then, that his basic survival traits are still strongly developed and, despite a relatively danger-free existence nowadays, still reverted to at moments of strong emotion or stress.

Domestication has been of more benefit to us than to the horse, and without him our history and development would have been greatly different. The horse made it possible for us to travel and trade, build and expand empires, wage wars and develop agriculture. His reward for all this is to enjoy a special place in our affections which has entailed the sacrifice of his freedom and the necessity of being kept in largely artificial surroundings ill-suited to the way in which he has evolved to survive.

Admittedly there are some benefits to be reaped for submitting to this captivity: domesticated horses live longer than free-living ones; a food supply is assured; there is freedom from predators; protection against, and treatment for, diseases and injuries; and shelter provided against the weather. It is unlikely that horses are aware of, or appreciate, these benefits – especially since, unless their owners are particularly knowledgeable, caring and conscientious, the reality is that they often suffer from a lack of exercise and company, an artificial and erratic diet, are bored by being stabled for long periods, and become insecure through insufficient natural social contact.

When considering the 'difficult' or 'problem' horse it is worth noting that free-living horses do not suffer from the behavioural problems exhibited by many domesticated equines. From the disease point of view, some ailments, such as laminitis and colic, are purely a result of domestication. For a horse to perform well for us, he needs to be both physically and mentally well and happy, relaxed and at ease in his surroundings and comfortable in his work. A lack of regard on the owner's or handler's part to any of these considerations is bound to lead ultimately to resistance, behavioural problems and vices.

The good horse manager will always bear in mind the horse's inherited natural characteristics, both physical and psychological; and, when devising a routine, will try to keep him in an environment which imitates that of nature as closely as it is reasonably practical to do so.

> The best horse care stems from an understanding of both the equine body and mind – it is not possible to entirely divorce the one from the other.

Environment

Today, the horse's environment is largely dictated by humans. Horses are what is termed 'trickle feeders'; although a great deal of the abdominal cavity is devoted to housing the digestive system, the stomach itself is relatively small in comparison to the overall size of the body, with a capacity of 21–25 pt (12–14l). Horses possess a genetically programmed grazing time of between twelve and sixteen hours a day; they are slow and selective eaters, working steadily away at the vegetation with mobile and active lips, picking out the choicest stems and plants. Their systems are especially adapted to deal with low-grade nutrients comprising large quantities of bulk and fibre, which is eaten and digested over long periods of time.

The digestive system works by means of a system of enzymes and specialized bacteria which break down and process the food. After a period of a few hours without any food, the bacteria start literally to starve to death. When the next food arrives, they are either weak or in insufficient numbers to digest it efficiently, which then leads to indigestion, unthriftiness or possibly colic.

It is natural for a horse to eat more or less continuously with short rest periods. In domestication the urge to graze still remains, but is suppressed. This suppression of the natural urge can exhibit itself in the form of bad doers, or horses described as temperamental and highly strung. Although a good horse manager will attempt to follow the golden rule of feeding little and often in order to duplicate natural grazing conditions, in practice this tends to consist of three concentrated feeds plus a haynet morning and evening. When remembering the amount of time that a horse is naturally accustomed to spending on eating, this is evidently a less satisfactory routine than

Fig 2 Horses living naturally spend much of their time grazing, possessing a genetically programmed grazing time of between twelve and sixteen hours a day.

might be supposed. The diet may be scientifically and carefully formulated to ensure that it is balanced, but it is still possible for the horse to be behaviourally if not physically underfed. There will be long periods during which the horse has nothing to do, and boredom will lead to stable vices such as crib-biting, windsucking, wood-chewing, rug-tearing, bed- and dung-eating as a substitute for grazing.

Concentrate feeds, whilst necessary to supply the energy which a horse may need to meet the increased demands that work places upon him, can be compared to the replacement meal food substitutes that we often use when dieting. Nutritionally, they may be perfect, but they are rarely as satisfying as a proper meal.

Ensuring that an ad lib supply of hay is available when a horse has to be stabled helps to keep him satisfied and occupied as well as ensuring that he receives an adequate proportion of the bulk and fibre needed in his diet to keep the digestive system functioning properly. In cases where a restricted diet is necessary – perhaps because of obesity, or a need to keep the horse lean in order to compete without placing undue stress on the limbs or internal organs – a haynet with small holes will stop him from eating his limited ration too quickly. The act of having to spend some time teasing the hay out will

also mimic, to a certain extent, the selective grazing habits he normally exhibits in the wild. Turning a horse out to graze in a paddock will also help; even if this can be managed for only a few hours, it is still better than nothing.

Much of the time, horses are kept stabled, which is a highly unsatisfactory state of affairs for the horse, who is basically a free-ranging animal. Stabling is largely a convenience for the owner, making it possible to segregate mares and stallions, and to keep the horse clean, dry and close at hand. It is easy to control the food intake to suit our requirements and produce an animal that is fit, and to keep him safe and secure.

Physically, this system subjects the horse to a dusty atmosphere, exposes him to draughts, extremes of temperature and interferes with natural lighting. Psychologically it disrupts the natural social patterns and interactions of herd life by isolating individuals for long periods of time leaving them with nothing to occupy themselves; and then imposes further stresses by mixing randomly selected groups together again, either out in the field or when ridden.

This is a pattern unlikely to change, because our own requirements dictate, and although horses do their best to adapt to their surroundings and routine, the

---

Stable vices

Free-living horses don't have them! Causes of vices may be:

- Boredom
- Digestive discomfort because of unnatural feeding routines
- Insecurity due to lack of equine companionship

- Insufficient exercise
- Insufficient freedom
- Lack of routine
- Stress of being confined in a stable for long periods

Fig 3 A horse turned out into a new paddock or exercise area will inspect his surroundings carefully, learning the shape and extent of his environment.

good horse manager will attempt to reach some kind of compromise. Some horses are better able to cope with confinement than others, but there is no doubt that most horses do best, both physically and emotionally, if they can be allowed out to graze in a paddock for some period of time during the day.

Even then, a paddock is a less satisfactory arrangement than might be supposed. In the wild, horses will range between thirty and eighty square miles in their search for food. In comparison, a couple of acres is a poor substitute for this, although it would obviously be impractical to manage large areas, and in most cases would be impossible to obtain them. For good grassland management as much as any other consideration, one acre per horse should be considered a minimum requirement.

When turning a horse out into a new paddock, you may notice him observing a ritual territorial patrol around the perimeter of the grazing area. This is called 'walking the fence', when the horse learns the shape and scope of the space before settling down to graze. Care should always be taken when introducing a new horse to a group of others, particularly when paddock space is limited. If an individual feels crowded, his desperate need for a larger territory may lead to a release of pent-up territorial aggression towards the newcomer, and he will attack (quite savagely in some instances) whom he considers to be the intruder. The attack may become quite serious and continued, despite repeated attempts at appeasement and submission on the newcomer's part. Fortunately, such attacks, with sensible management, are not too common since horses are by and large peaceable animals amongst their own kind. Nevertheless the fact remains that they are complex beings in the company of other horses, and in such circumstances may exhibit unexpected characteristics, regardless of how well trained they may be by the owner or handler.

Affection and Intelligence

Horses are highly sociable animals; very much gregarious by nature, they suffer if kept in isolation from each other. A group of horses out in a field together will develop their own pecking order, but status is by no means inflexible: for example, a dominant horse will quickly lose his position if he is feeling below par and run down.

They may develop strong bonds of affection for each other. Sometimes a very strong friendship beteen two animals will be noticed, and this can prove to be a problem if one decides that he does not want to leave the company of the other. In situations where horses are overcrowded, however, there may be frequent bouts of bickering, and even the strongest of friendships may deteriorate.

Displays of affection between horses are most commonly expressed by bouts of mutual grooming. For a foal, having his coat gently nibbled by his mother symbolizes moments of peace, security, and maternal love, and as an adult the association between grooming and affection is retained. Delicate nibbling movements made by the front teeth help to remove matted and dead hairs, and enable the horse to relieve himself of itches that he cannot normally reach by himself. Scratching against a fence post or tree

Fig 4 Mutual grooming.

trunk is an alternative solution but is less accurate and subtle.

The more friendly two horses are, the more frequently they will indulge in mutual grooming. Facing head to tail, they will often work their way along the crest of the neck and down to the base of the withers. Most often it is the more submissive of the two who approaches and initiates the grooming, and the dominant one who decides when to end the session. A horse owner can make use of this characteristic, using his fingers to imitate the action of the teeth; it is a more subtle and understandable gesture to the horse than the hearty slapping and patting of necks which normally goes on, and it is not unusual to find the gesture being reciprocated!

Horses are not tremendously intelligent and they lack powers of imagination and foresight, but they do possess limited powers of reasoning and logic. Hence, some are able to learn how to undo bolts on stable doors and let themselves out, or how to pull the loose end of a lead rope and untie themselves. They also have excellent memories, an essential requisite for an animal who enjoys a wide variety of different plants and must remember and be able to distinguish between those which taste good or unpleasant, or are poisonous. We make extensive use of this trait when training horses, but to counter this benefit to us, they have a highly developed instinct for self-preservation, which can often take precedence over trained obedience to a human's commands.

Their long memories can also have another disadvantage for us, in that unpleasant experiences or associations are retained for many years: a handler or rider may suddenly encounter resistance or a problem for which he can find no readily discernible reason or cause, but which has its roots in the distant past.

> *Do not confuse equine and human intelligence, and respect both . . .*
>
> (Charles Harris)

Communication

Unlike humans, horses have no real capacity for lying, although they may attempt to call our bluff on occasion! They are able to communicate their desires, intentions and emotional state quite clearly to other horses through their posture and a limited series of vocalizations, perhaps an apparent and unmistakable threat or a more subtle gesture

such as a slight wrinkling of the nostrils in disgust.

If the handler or rider is observant and prepared to devote a little time to studying each of the individual animals in his care, he will find that this body language can provide an invaluable guide to the horse's frame of mind, and will enable him to judge whether a difficult horse is merely trying it on, is in deadly earnest, or perhaps misbehaving because he is in pain. With some understanding of how the horse communicates, it is possible for the handler or rider to anticipate a problem and to deal with it either more sympathetically or firmly, as the situation indicates.

> Quite often the clues are all there: the rider/handler must simply be alert enough to spot them, and smart enough to interpret them correctly.

Ears

The horse is finely attuned to the environment he lives in; he has had to be in order to survive. As a result, he has a very keen sense of hearing, which enables him to detect the presence of possible predators in the vicinity. The ears are funnel-shaped, and controlled by around sixteen muscles so that they can be rotated to pinpoint precisely the source of particular sounds. The ears are seldom still and they perform a dual role: they are an early warning system and a means of communicating the emotional state.

Relaxed ears
When the horse is relaxed and secure in

Fig 5 Totally relaxed and dozing, ears held loosely, lower lip drooping, and eyes closed.

his surroundings, the ears are held loosely with the openings pointing forwards and outwards in a listening mode, absorbing the sounds around him. The moment a strange or unexpected noise is heard, one or both ears swivel towards it for a more careful examination.

Pricked ears

Pricked ears indicate general alertness and interest, but ears are also pricked when the horse has been startled or if he is being especially vigilant. They will also be observed when one horse first approaches to greet another. The ears will become stiffly pricked when any strange or worrying sound is heard; the whole head and possibly the body will also turn in order to focus better on the source of alarm.

Drooping ears

Ears that are drooping, with the openings facing down towards the ground, are a sign of a tired or exhausted horse; by showing no interest in what is going on around him, the animal shows that he is feeling mentally as well as physically drained. A more extreme example of this switching off from all incoming messages may occur when the horse is very sleepy (or sedated) or in pain. Drooping ears may also be used to signal submission during stressful social encounters or status battles, a sign that the horse is giving in to his social superior.

Erect, busy ears

Anxiety or panic may be indicated by busily twitching erect ears, quickly flicking back and forth. This should not be confused with the horse casually flicking an ear back to listen to the rider or handler.

Ears turned backwards

This is sometimes observed in a horse who is very much dominated by the rider; he is signalling his submission by turning the ear opening towards the rider in order to catch any tiny sound.

Flattened ears

This is a clear sign of aggression or dominance, and is often accompanied by an ugly experession. It is also a self-defence posture; since ears are easily bitten and torn in attacks, pinning them back is the safest way of holding them.

Fig 6 Anxious and unsettled.

Face

The face cannot manage to convey complex or elaborate nuances of expression, but can indicate shifting moods.

Eyes

Generally they should be open and clear, with a kindly expression. If they are half-closed it may be because the horse is relaxed, probably dozing, or to indicate submissiveness; fully closed eyes may be a sign of exhaustion or pain. Eyes opened wider than usual are an indication of fear, anxiety or apprehension (very much as they are with humans). When opened very wide, possibly showing some white around the rims, it is usually a sign of anger or aggression (don't be misled by a horse who has a small iris and permanently shows some white in his eye!).

Nostrils

The nostrils may be wrinkled to show disgust, and are flared when excited or feeling some intense emotion (so as to draw more air into the lungs and prepare for flight if necessary). Flehmen, the curling up of the top lip to expose the upper teeth and gums, giving the horse the appearance that he is laughing, is often shown by horses who are sexually aroused or experiencing an unusual or unpleasant smell or taste. It is thought that this curling of the upper lip helps to trap air in the nasal cavities, forcing it to circulate more deeply so that the horse can consider it more carefully, just as we might sniff deeply at the aroma of cooking so as to appreciate it better.

Lips

A drooping lower lip is characteristic of a very relaxed, sleepy, tired or exhausted horse. If the lips are stiff and tight, it is usually caused by tension, anxiety, pain or fear, and can probably best be compared to a human pursing, biting, or pressing their lips together.

Bite threat

The jaws are held tensely open, with the teeth fully exposed. The threat alone (usually accompanied by flattened ears and wide eyes) is often enough to see off an opponent without any contact being made.

Nose nudging

A nudge from a nose can be a sign of the horse seeking attention or, at the opposite extreme, he may actually lunge at another horse or person in an aggressive manner, possibly when he is about to bite. Both gestures are assertive statements.

Neck

Headshaking

Headshaking is a natural reaction when flies land on the horse's face, and is one of the ways in which he will attempt to rid himself of the nuisance. When irritated or frustrated, he may act as though trying to shake off flies, tossing and jerking the head to remove whatever is annoying him, perhaps the bit, or an unsympathetic rein contact.

Weaving

This is a term used to describe the side-to-side swinging action of the head and neck. In extreme cases, the horse will actually rock from foot to foot. It is not a natural action and is never observed in wild horses. Such a habit should alert the horse owner or manager to the fact that there is something wrong or lacking in the horse's environment. It is a means of relieving boredom, usually caused by over-confinement and a lack of exercise and stimulus.

Body Posture

Much in the horse's body posture can be related to the human's. The more elevated it is, the more excited, generally speaking, the horse is; the head and tail will be held high and the strides will be light and airy (in the same way as a human will walk with a certain spring in his step). A horse who is making a declaration of superiority will give an appearance of growing taller and standing proudly, whilst one who is depressed, tired or submissive will do the opposite and slump (just as a human will).

Presenting quarters

Swinging the quarters around to face some kind of threat is a defensive display, implying that a kick from the back feet is likely to follow if provoked further.

Body blocking

Turning the body in front of another horse is another form of threat, although less extreme than actually presenting the quarters. By placing the other animal in a position where he must either challenge or submit in order to pass, he reinforces his status. A more intense form of challenge involving physical contact takes place when the horse uses his shoulders to barge against and push aside another. It goes without saying that an alert person will be aware of the deeper message implicit in a horse who persists in pushing or shoving at the handler; this is very important if the relationship is to remain on the correct footing.

Legs

Pawing at the ground

Pawing or scraping at the ground with a forefoot is, in origin, a movement associated with feeding, and is also a means of investigating the ground. It is usually exhibited by a horse who has a strong desire to move forward, but is being frustrated by something physically preventing it, such as a stable door or a rider insisting that he stands still.

Lifting a front leg

A threat is implied by this gesture, which is a milder version of what happens when a horse actually fights, striking out with his front feet.

Fig 7 The tail serves a practical function as a fly switch, and horses turned out together will often be observed standing head to tail during the summer months to help keep flies at bay more efficiently.

Lifting a back foot
This is normally defensive as opposed to aggressive; a kick may follow.

Stamping
Stamping a foot is a modified form of kicking. It is a mildly threatening gesture when the horse is irritated, maybe by a rider saddling up or tightening the girths.

> *Do not play about with horses – their teeth and hooves have immeasurable impact . . .*
>
> (Charles Harris)

Tail

The tail serves a very practical function as a fly switch in addition to providing a useful key to the horse's frame of mind. When he is relaxed and comfortable, the tail will be held loosely; when working, it will be carried slightly away from the quarters and moving with a gentle swing.

High
The tail held high is an indication of alertness; a horse who has been startled by something will be seen to lift his tail and will probably move away from the supposed threat with a characteristically

elevated stride. When playing, the tail will also be lifted, often as high as possible. If the horse has been frightened by something, he is quite likely to evacuate his bowels at the same time, so as to lighten himself as much as possible prior to taking flight. A mare who is in season will also carry her tail high as an invitation to other horses, holding it to one side and winking with her vulva.

Clamped down

At the other extremes, a tail which is clamped tightly down may signal that a kick is about to be delivered, or if ridden, that a buck might be forthcoming. A clamped-down tail can also indicate temper, resistance and general tension (perhaps related to pain) in the back when being ridden.

Swishing tail

Not to be confused with a relaxed tail which is flicking casually at flies, one which is swished violently generally denotes anger, but also possibly discomfort if being ridden.

Crooked tail

A tail which is habitually carried to one side when the horse is ridden may be a sign of crookedness and/or back trouble.

Vocal Signals

Horses do not have an elaborate vocal language, and such vocalization as they do employ is not always used rigidly in a single context with a single meaning. Together with general grunts and groans of exertion, and occasional sighs of boredom, the vocal language such as it is, can be loosely categorized into six groups:

Snorting

Snorting indicates wariness. The action of snorting clears the airways ready for action, whilst the noise helps to alert other herd members to possible danger. The head and tail are usually held high, with the body showing unmistakable signs of tenseness and excitement. The horse may also snort when there is a conflict between curiosity and fear, such as meeting a strange object when out hacking, or when two strange horses meet each other and their mutual interest is tinged with anxiety until social status has been established.

Blowing

Less violent than snorting, this is more of an exhalation of air, with a meaning which can extend from curiosity to a simple statement of satisfaction.

Squeal

A defensive signal used during aggressive encounters, it indicates that the horse has been pushed quite far enough and further aggravation will result in retaliation of some kind.

Neigh

The loudest and longest of sounds a horse makes, a neigh starts as a squeal and ends as a nicker. It is the equine equivalent of a dog howling: it is a demand for information when isolated, or perhaps when spotting another horse in the distance.

Roar

A horse roaring or screaming in rage or fear at another one is an unmistakable signal of the horse's aggressive intentions; it is most likely to be heard in an encounter between stallions.

Fig 8 How not to lead! Even small ponies can be surprisingly strong and should be treated with as much respect and awareness of safety as larger horses. Note the handler's lack of concentration and gloves, and the lead rope wrapped tightly around the hand. It is at moments such as this that accidents invariably happen.

Nicker

A low-pitched guttural nicker is a friendly greeting signal used at close quarters when a friend (or an owner, perhaps with a feed bucket!) is recognized. A courtship nicker is similar, but longer and lower pitched in tone with very definite sexual connotations, whilst a maternal nicker used by a mare to her foal when she is mildly concerned about him is very soft, and barely audible.

Survival Traits – The Senses

In the past, the horse's survival has depended largely upon his ability to sense danger and then to flee swiftly from it; only when there is no other option and the horse is unable to make his escape will he turn to fight. As a result, he has a highly developed early-warning system, which can sometimes be used to our advantage, but equally, is just as likely to create problems for a handler or rider lacking in understanding. The senses upon which the horse relies to relay information about his immediate environment are sight, hearing, smell, taste and touch.

Sight

The horse's eyes are large in comparison to the human's. Situated as they are on the side of the face, they allow a fairly wide band of all-round vision – about 340 of the 360 degrees around him. Whilst equine vision is less detailed than ours, it is far more sensitive to even the tiniest of movements: he can easily be panicked by a sudden movement on the edge of his range of vision. This could provide one of the reasons why young horses can become so tense and anxious when mounted for the first time: they cannot see the rider, just odd peripheral movements. Combine this with the fact that the rider could easily be interpreted in the horse's mind as being a predator leaping onto his back, and it is humbling to realize the amount of courage and trust an essentially timid animal places in his human trainers.

There are two small blind spots, just in front of, and immediately behind, the body, which is why it is important never to approach even a well-trained and sensible horse directly from the rear without first giving some warning. Even so, it is still best to approach from the side! Because the eyes are set to the sides of the head, the horse normally sees things as lacking in perspective. If you close one eye, you will obtain a similar view. There is a narrow band of three-dimensional vision when looking directly ahead, but because of the length of the face, this vision only works at a distance of about four to six feet or more in front of the head.

This is perhaps more easily understood if you compare it with trying to see an object directly in front of the tip of your nose – and it is considerably easier for a human, with eyes set to the front.

This means that when jumping, the horse is in effect tackling an obstacle 'blind': he can see the fence whilst approaching but, at the last moment, it disappears from view, blocked out by the length of his head. Again, it is a tribute to the horse's courage, and the faith he places in the rider, that he is willing to jump at all; and the fact that he is jumping from memory might explain why occasionally he will make a real hash of a seemingly straightforward obstacle.

As a result of a light-intensifying device within the eye, a layer which reflects light back onto the retina, the horse is better than the rider at seeing in dimly lit conditions. His eyes adjust less quickly than the human's to abrupt changes in light intensity, however, so he may hesitate before moving from light to shade – a point to bear in mind when jumping cross-country fences sited in shady areas, or when leading a horse into a dark stable.

Hearing

Equine hearing is considerably better than that of humans, with the added ability to detect a wide range of sounds, from very high to very low frequencies. The ears are constantly moving to pick up new sounds and pin-point their sources, but a noisy environment can prove to be immensely distressing. Horses can block out sounds to a degree by flattening their ears, but this only provides a minimum of relief. Noises that are loud for us must be almost unbearable for horses, with their greater sensitivity to noise; the practice of playing loud music on the radio in many stable yards may help to jolly the staff along with their work, but is hardly conducive to producing a settled, relaxed horse. Similarly, sudden, loud noises, such as mucking out tools being dropped or doors being slammed, will startle and alarm the horse.

There are some benefits to such sensitivity however, not least being the pleasure an owner feels when the horse recognizes his step approaching the stable. More usefully, the handler or rider can often obtain a good response by use of the voice. A low tone, with long drawn-out syllables can be immensely soothing to an agitated or anxious horse, whilst a brisk, authoritative voice will convey the message that no nonsense will be stood for. In the case of an idle or inattentive horse, commands given with a rising inflection will often work wonders. It should be remembered that the horse will detect just as quickly uncertainty, lack of confidence or fear in the handler's or rider's tone.

Smell

Smell is an important sense, enabling the horse to detect predators, and stallions to tell when a mare is coming into heat. A mare will use scent to identify her foal. Smell is also a means of identifying other individuals: when a strange horse approaches another, they will sniff at each other with extreme care, blowing gently into the nostrils.

It is not a wise idea to allow horses to touch noses and indulge in this form of greeting when being ridden or led, however, as having made each other's acquaintance they may discover that they

Fig 9 Mares use scent to enable them to identify their own offspring.

are potential rivals: a squeal will frequently follow, accompanied perhaps by the threat of a nip or striking out with a foreleg, which is dangerous for the handlers or riders.

The delicacy of the horse's sense of smell is often brought home to the handler when changing to a different brand of feedstuff, or attempting to add medicines or wormer to the feed. It is not unusual for the horse to detect the difference and to turn his nose up at it! Neither does it take long for him to associate the vet's visits with the smell of antiseptic or disinfectant on his clothing. Strong or unusual smells can also create problems: horses often refuse to go near, or pass them – pigs are commonly a cause of such behaviour, even if they cannot be seen or heard.

One way of trying to deal with such problems – and not unknown to the horse 'whisperers' of the past, who claimed to have special powers over horses – is to try and confuse the sense of smell by smearing a strong-smelling ointment onto the muzzle: a little menthol vapour rub smeared onto the false nostril often does the trick. This can also be tried when trying to foster an orphan foal onto another mare; ordinarily, his smell would be wrong and she would be inclined to reject it.

Taste

Horses have an excellent sense of taste, which, combined with their well-developed sense of smell and mobile lips can enable them to pick out more palatable food from less pleasant substances such as worming powders added to the feeds. Most horses seem to have a sweet tooth, but also relish sour and bitter tastes, too.

Touch

The horse's sense of touch is as well developed as a human's: he feels pain as keenly, can feel the touch of something as light as a fly landing on his body (despite a layer of hair covering the skin), and enjoys pleasurable tactile sensations such as having a difficult-to-reach itch scratched. The muzzle is especially sensitive, and is used in much the same way as a human will use fingers to investigate objects, and with the nostrils, lips and tongue placed close together, the horse can gather a great deal of information. In dark or poorly lit areas, the long whiskers around the muzzle (and eyes) also assist him in discovering the proximity of solid objects around him. For this reason, many people now leave them alone, although many of the showing fraternity persist in trimming them off for cosmetic reasons.

Sixth Sense

Often mocked and sneered at is the idea that animals, horses included, possess a 'sixth sense'. While much of this may be put down to the horse's highly tuned senses of smell and hearing, they do seem to be aware of approaching weather conditions, and to be sensitive to magnetic fields. Horses moved to earthquake zones, for example, have been uneasy initially and taken some time to settle. Whether horses really possess a sixth sense or not remains a topic open to much dispute.

Herd Instinct

In the wild, horses tend to band together into small herds for reasons of safety as

Fig 10 The herd instinct can be exploited by a rider in certain cases, in this instance taking a lead from another horse.

much as through any desire for social intercourse. With more members in a herd, a greater number of 'lookouts' are available to warn of approaching danger. This instinct to remain with other horses can present problems, but can also be utilized by using one horse as a 'school-master' to introduce another horse to, and reassure him about, new experiences and activities.

The Handler/Rider

To train or handle a horse successfully requires knowledge, patience, sympathy, skill, and confidence: a good handler or rider must be quiet, determined, good tempered, and possess an ability to see things from the horse's point of view. An appreciation of what makes the horse tick – both psychologically and anatomically – is essential when attempting to deal with any horse, and especially when confronted with a problem animal. A lack of understanding of either can soon lead to evasions and vices.

The handler or rider should also possess the ability to recognize and differentiate between nervousness, confusion and genuine naughtiness or bad manners, as each requires different handling. Anticipation of factors which may cause problems, as much as anticipation of a particular evasion can be vital. Horses have limited powers of reasoning, and obedience to the handler or rider is instilled by forming habits through repetition, association and reward. Bad habits are as easily learnt as good ones, and each time the horse succeeds in getting the better of the handler, he will attempt to repeat the evasion in order to avoid work or doing something he does not wish to. However, the habit of obedience can be overridden by pain or fear, when instinctive behaviour

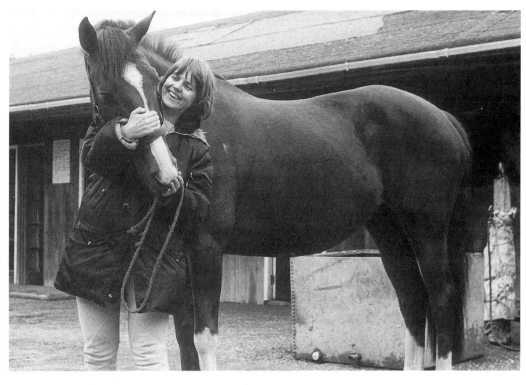

Fig 11 Establishing a good rapport with the horse is vital, and allowances need to be made for individual temperaments. This horse enjoys a fuss and is clearly quite extrovert, but some horses hate to be treated like this.

will take the upper hand. Pain should, as far as possible, be avoided as a means of training: rather, the handler should attempt to overcome the horse's natural timidity and fear by gaining his trust and confidence.

Discipline is required on occasion, and while quiet kindness has an important role, there are times when it is not always the most appropriate method and the handler may sometimes find it necessary to be quite aggressively firm. However,

Handler/rider qualities:

- Observation
- 'Feel'
- Patience
- Perseverance
- Riding and handling competence

- Quietness
- Firmness
- Tact
- Knowledge

Fig 12 Natural timidity and fear needs to be overcome by gaining the horse's confidence. This part of his education should begin as early as possible in his life.

Fig 13 A good instructor with an understanding of equine psychology can often be a real asset when dealing with problem horses.

the handler must beware of losing his temper, which can lead to a loss of rational thought and unnecessarily severe and punishing action. When punishment is necessary, this should be carried out at the immediate time of the incident: punishment after the event is largely useless because the horse will not understand the reason for it and will as a result become bad tempered and distrustful.

The handler should also appreciate that there is a time and a place for everything, and that there is no point in trying to teach new lessons if the horse is tired, fresh or over-excited, although quite often when evasions or resistances do crop up it is not always possible to choose the time or the place.

Identifying the cause of a problem and trying to differentiate between genuine anxiety or naughtiness can sometimes be a tall order, and often it helps to seek the services of a good instructor with an understanding of equine psychology – never allow pride to get in the way of the horse's welfare.

> *My horses understand me tolerably well . . . they live in great amity with me . . .*
>
> (Jonathan Swift)

CHAPTER 2

Handling the Horse

Obviously it is far more pleasant to deal with a tractable, amenable horse than one who is snappy or plain bolshy, particularly since an owner or handler is likely to find himself spending more hours caring for the horse from the ground than actually in the saddle riding him.

Teaching the horse good manners and what is required of him is something that can be begun just a few days after birth when he can be taught to wear a headcollar and to submit to being handled and led; this can require great patience as well as a degree of firmness when necessary (but never coercion, which might create a troublesome animal later in life). It is far more sensible for the handler to begin these lessons early when the horse is still relatively weak and less able to put up physical resistance than later on in his life when he has reached full strength. Discipline, obedience, and deference to the handler are habits which should be cultivated right from the start so that the horse does not learn to question and rebel against human authority, whether on the ground or when under saddle. It should be remembered, however, that many of the things we expect horses to do are not natural to him, and resistances should be met by the handler with understanding rather than brute force. The handler should seek to reassure the horse, giving him time to understand each lesson and not expect or demand too

much of him too soon. A successful partnership will be based on mutual respect and trust, not on fear; a frightened horse will always create problems in some respect.

Sadly, some horses do actually become vicious as opposed to merely difficult, frequently as a result of an unnatural lifestyle combined with bad handling. Such horses can be a real danger to all those who have to handle them and cannot safely be allowed to remain in an environment where novices or children are likely to come into contact with them. No matter what precautions may be taken, the safety of humans must take first priority, and accidents can happen at any time.

While such horses may be tolerated if they are of great stud value or exceptionally talented as competition horses, they require firm and understanding handling by an experienced horseman. Some cases may be reformed but it is a time-consuming process, and it is never entirely wise, even so, to trust him completely thereafter. It should also be noted that dealing forcefully with such horses rarely meets with success, breeding only further distrust and ill temper.

Refusal to Back

Occasionally, the handler may wish to manoeuvre the horse into a certain posi-

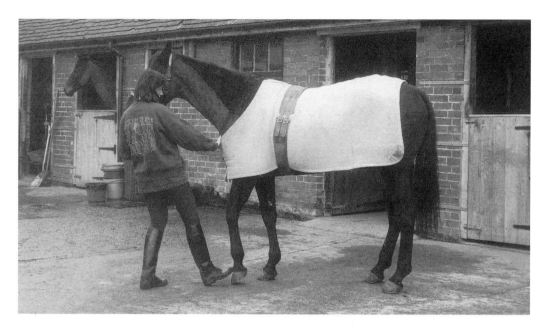

Fig 14 A tap on the coronet with the toe of one foot, combined with a hand pushing against the chest will usually encourage the horse to move backwards. Do not stand directly in front of him however, in case he strikes out with a forefoot or tries to move forward instead.

tion, or simply push him back from a stable door while the handler enters or leaves the box. Not only should the horse defer to the handler and move over when asked, but also move backwards when required. This can be an awkward manoeuvre for some horses, particularly if they suffer from back problems. If resistance is still met with after the following methods are tried, pain should not be ruled out, and the horse should be thoroughly checked over by a veterinary surgeon.

When asking the horse to move backwards, stand slightly to the front and to one side of him. Placing one hand on the chest, push firmly and repeat the command 'Back'. If there is no response, a tap from the toe of one boot on the front of the horse's coronet, combined with the above,

Fig 15 Using a lead rope to encourage the horse to back up.

will usually encourage him to move backwards away from the pressure. Alternatively, passing a piece of rope across the front of the face midway between the eyes and nostrils and then exerting a backwards and slight side-to-side sawing movement on it should obtain the desired effect.

Biting

Being bitten is never a pleasant experience, although it can be common amongst entire male horses and ponies since it is one of the ways in which they exert their dominance over other members of their herd and any rivals. Biting or nipping may be a way of the horse showing his superiority over humans, but can also be an aggressive act, or one of self-defence.

Some horses may be nervous rather than downright nasty, but in either instance the habit must be dealt with firmly and correction meted out instantly. Repeating the command 'No' sharply, the horse should be smacked on the neck, avoiding the head as this may make him

> **Safety:** Always ensure there is plenty of room to the rear of the horse, and that there are no jutting projections on which he might catch a hip if he moves crookedly. Never stand directly in front of the horse in case he attempts to push forwards, or rear.

Fig 16 Biting is common amongst entire male horses and ponies, being one of the ways in which they exert their dominance over other members of the herd.

Fig 17 Tougher tactics may be needed with a horse who actually lunges
forwards with his jaws open and a threatening look on his face. (Photo: Mike Wood)

headshy. The handler should not continue to punish the horse unnecessarily as it is likely to make him defensive.

Other than dealing with the problem when it arises, the handler should try to avoid putting the horse in a situation that will encourage biting or nipping – for example, when tightening girths and rollers, or grooming ticklish or sensitive areas. If it is the handler who is the cause of discomfort, it is not surprising if the horse tries to retaliate. If the horse is known to nip – perhaps from anticipation of discomfort – he should be tied up short so that he cannot reach to bite. However, this should not be used as an excuse to continue causing the horse discomfort; it is quite likely that if this does happen and the horse cannot use his teeth, he may resort to cow-kicking instead.

There are a few individuals whose tendency to use their teeth goes beyond the occasional (sometimes deserved) nip. In the case of a horse who actually lunges towards the handler, with jaws open and a threatening look on his face, tougher tactics may be in order. First of all, the management of the horse should be considered — whether he is receiving enough freedom and exercise and is being fairly treated by the handler are important points. A horse who is this dangerous is unsuitable for an inexperienced person to handle, and any nervousness on the handler's part will quickly be detected by the horse and lead to a rapid deterioration of the situation. The handler must be continually on the alert while handling the horse and, should he attempt to lunge at him, it is justifiable to carry a short stick and administer a sharp smack on the end of the nose with it. Having made the point, the handler should not lay into the horse with the stick, as it will only cause further resentment of humans in general and can turn the problem horse into a seriously savage one, which eventually nobody will be prepared to handle.

While on the subject of biting or nipping, it is worth thinking about the role of titbits in the horse's training and daily management. The occasional titbit will do no harm and can be a useful incentive in some cases, such as when catching a horse out in the field, but, as with all things, moderation is advisable. Horses who are indiscriminately fed titbits soon come to expect them as a matter of course, and should one not be forthcoming, or the supply finished, it may nip out of irritation, or attempt to bully the handler into producing more goodies. Praise is often a more suitable reward than food although, in some instances, bribery may be justified. The handler should also remember the dangers inherent in offering titbits to a horse in view of others, which can provoke jealousy and aggressive behaviour.

> **Safety**: Wear a padded jacket, or some kind of clothing which offers protection to the arms.

Fig 18 Indiscriminate feeding of titbits is inadvisable.

Chewing

Youngsters quite often go through a phase of chewing – clothing, wooden projections in the stable or fencing – while they are teething. Asking the vet for a preparation to rub on the gums to alleviate soreness may help, and all wooden structures can be treated with a proprietary brand of unpleasant-tasting preparation to discourage the horse from doing any further damage. Clothing can be protected by using a bib (see Rug Tearing, page 79) or applying bitter aloes, available from chemists, although the latter does stain.

Lead ropes may also come in for attention when the horse is tied up; some horses may express irritation or discomfort by biting at it when being groomed. Ultimately, this will lead to a damaged lead rope and also, perhaps, to the horse learning how to untie himself. The easiest solution is to use a chain with a spring-clip at each end instead of a rope, although it should be attached to a piece of breakable twine rather than directly to a fixed ring because, if the horse pulls back for some reason, they can be difficult to release quickly.

Grooming kits and so forth should not be left lying around in the stable, and any attempts to chew the handler's clothing should be firmly discouraged by pushing the head away and sternly repeating the command 'No!'

Fig 19 Youngsters often go through a phase of chewing, which can be a destructive and expensive habit.

Clipping

Clipping is not essential, but if the horse is expected to work reasonably hard during the winter months, it will allow him to do so without becoming unduly distressed; it also makes it easier to cool and dry him off after exercise, with less danger of chilling.

Not all horses particularly relish the experience, particularly if they have been badly handled or nicked when being clipped in the past. Similarly, if he has been clipped while damp or with blunt blades, the clippers will have pulled at the hair, leaving the horse with painful memories, which can certainly make him apprehensive and restless if not downright difficult to clip in the future.

Even if the horse has not actually suffered discomfort while being clipped, the noise of the machine can be as frightening for the horse as the unaccustomed vibration against the skin. It is worth trying to stable a young horse near to the clipping area in the yard so that he can become used to the sound before he is clipped for the first time. Using a grooming machine can also help him to adjust to the new experience. Horses who are distressed by the noise may find the whole operation more tolerable if they first have a chunk of cotton wool placed in each ear to help muffle the sound a little.

It might also help to try using clippers with a less powerful motor as these are generally quieter and generate less vibration. The very small, rechargeable or battery-operated clippers of the type used by dog beauticians can also be worth trying,

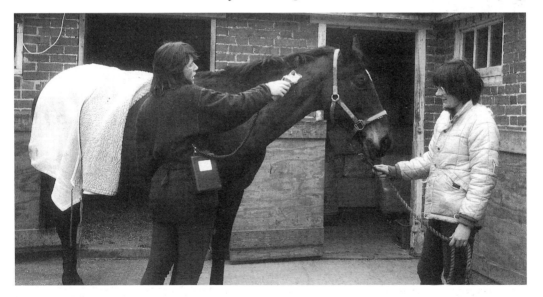

Fig 20 A clipper cable can be a potential source of anxiety for many horses. Using clippers which operate from a portable power pack can be very helpful in such instances. The model shown here is the Lister 'Showman' which also has an advantage over conventional mains-powered clippers in that it is much quieter.

particularly in more difficult areas such as around the head and ears. Many awkward horses will tolerate this type of clipper, which is lighter and easier to manoeuvre, although the narrower blades will make it a longer task.

Hand clippers can provide an alternative to powered ones, but can be very tiring for the handler to use, and can make the whole operation very time consuming.

A potential source of anxiety for many horses is the clipper cable itself if they are mains-powered: sudden movements of it can startle the horse, and will be an additional hazard anyway if he is already restless or worried. Clippers which operate from a portable battery pack slung from the handler's waist can be a real asset since they do away with the need for a long, trailing cable which may not just be frightening to the horse, but may be trodden on or become entangled with the handler's feet. Just as importantly, it enables the handler to move more freely around the horse, making it possible to reduce the actual clipping time.

One other factor that might be considered when confronted with a difficult horse is environment. Some are better to clip out of doors (weather permitting) than in a stable where they may feel hemmed in and threatened. Others may be safer inside a stable, where they are unable to drag the handler off across the yard. It is a case of deciding what is best for the individual horse.

If it is essential that the horse is clipped, but real problems are experienced, which could make the procedure hazardous to either horse or handler, some method of restraint could be used, such as a twitch. Should this prove to be unsuccessful, the only other option is to ask the vet to sedate the horse (see Appendix I, page 153).

Crowding

Horses who shove against the handler, pushing him out of the way or crushing him against a stable wall or partition, exhibit a lack of respect for the handler's authority and are asserting their own dominance and superiority. It may be due to ignorance of stable manners because of his young age, in which case a smack on the belly and a sharp reprimand usually teaches him better. The handler should always insist that the horse give way to him and move on command when asked to. Keeping the horse's head turned slightly towards the handler when pushing his quarters over makes it more difficult for the horse to resist when a hand is pressed against his hip.

Older horses who have become confirmed in this habit can be discouraged by the handler's carrying a stout stick slightly longer than the width of the handler's body. When a horse attempts to crush the handler against the wall, one end of the stick can be wedged against it and the

Safety: The horse should be clean and dry, the clipper blades sharp and correctly tensioned (the manufacturer's instructions will tell the handler how to check this). The clippers should be earthed, and the horse standing on a dry, non-slip surface. An assistant should be available to hold the horse, rather than tying him up. Always take care with the clipper mains lead (if any), keeping it out of the way of both horse and handler's feet.

other end held against the horse's body, and a sharp reprimand given. Once the horse realizes that such tactics only result in discomfort for him, he will soon desist from the habit altogether.

Feet – Difficult to Pick Up

The horse should be taught to tolerate having his feet picked up while he is young, but some horses persist in being awkward about it. Allowances should be made for youngsters who will initially find it difficult to balance on three legs for very long and who may attempt to slam the held foot back down again as they begin to tire or if they lose their balance. Older horses, who have become stiff or arthritic in their joints, and those suffering from back problems may also experience some discomfort when the feet are picked up, making them unco-operative. Care should therefore be taken to avoid picking the feet up too high, or holding them up for too long, otherwise trouble is bound to ensue. Pulling the hind legs too far out to the side can also cause discomfort as well as loss of balance, since the joints are not designed to articulate in such a manner.

A horse who flatly refuses to pick his feet up can be encouraged to do so by the handler standing close to him and grasping the fetlock joint firmly while leaning against the horse's shoulder or flank; this will make the horse transfer his weight onto the other three legs, making it easier to pick up the fourth. If the horse will still not pick his foot up, pinching the area between the base of the cannon bone and tendon just above the fetlock joint, between finger and thumb, while contin-

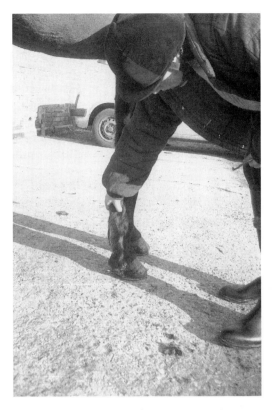

Fig 21 Using finger and thumb to pinch the area above the fetlock joint between bone and tendon to encourage the horse to pick his foot up.

uing to lean against his side usually does the trick. If the horse attempts to put his foot straight down again, support the hoof with one hand and keep the joints flexed. Leaning slightly against the horse is a useful ploy to use if he tends to lean onto the handler's hands.

If the horse has a tendency to kick out, the handler should be careful that he is not to blame for the reaction, especially with more nervous types. Grabbing at the fetlock joint with no warning is likely to startle him into a defensive action; so when picking up a forefoot, the handler

Fig 22 Picking up the hind feet should be done with care. Here, the handler demonstrates the incorrect way, with her arm passing behind the leg.

Fig 23 The correct way to pick up a foot.

should start by stroking slowly down the neck, working gradually down to the shoulder, foreleg and finally to the fetlock joint. The same procedure should be followed when picking up a hind foot, stroking from the neck, along the back and quarters down to the hock joint and then to the fetlock. The handler should stand close to the horse, so that if he does kick, the handler will be pushed away, rather than receive the full force of the blow. Keeping the joints flexed will also

Safety: The handler should wear gloves to give protection to the hands, and sensible footwear to afford some protection to the toes should the horse put his foot down abruptly. When picking up the hind feet, the hoof should be supported from the inside of the limb, not with the arm passing behind it. In this last posture, the arm is in a stressed position and, should the horse kick out, a dislocated shoulder may result. Held correctly, in such a situation, the arm will follow in the direction of the kick instead.

help to stop the horse from kicking, and in the case of a hind leg, it can be drawn out slightly to the side (but not so much as to cause discomfort) so that the horse is slightly off-balance and more likely to put his foot down than to kick with it. (*See also* Shoeing Difficulties page 50.)

Grooming Difficulties

Most horses who are difficult to groom are only so as a result of thoughtless and rough handling. Using stiff-bristled brushes on ticklish areas such as the belly, head and between the legs will irritate, especially if the horse is clipped, and banging the back of a brush against bony parts will also cause discomfort. Some horses are especially sensitive and special care may need to be taken, avoiding the use of harsh-bristled brushes and plastic curry combs. Very sensitive areas are probably best dealt with using either a damp sponge in the summer, or a soft stable rubber, or even just the fingers to gently tease out persistent clinging patches patches of mud. It will take a little longer, but will pay off in the long term in that the horse will learn that he is not going to be hurt, and will gain trust and confidence.

If the horse is one who is inclined to nip, he should be tied up short and perhaps given a haynet to keep his mind occupied, but the fact that he is tied up and cannot retaliate should not be an excuse for careless and hasty grooming.

Headshyness

Headshyness is usually due to fear, pain, or perhaps a combination of both. Re-grettably, far too many horses display this problem to a greater or lesser extent. The horse will resent having his head handled, and usually attempts to evade the handler's efforts to touch it by placing it as high in the air as possible. Obviously this causes problems when attempting to bridle or groom the horse, and remedying it will take much patience.

Horses who have been beaten around the head will display signs of fear; or pain may have been caused by a badly fitting bit or bridle. Most horses are startled by rapid, abrupt movements, and if these are repeatedly made around the head area,

Fig 24 Take extra care when grooming the head, using a soft cloth, sponge or just fingers if necessary, avoiding rough or sudden movements.

the horse may become wary, even though he may not actually have experienced pain. Horses have a very retentive memory, particularly for distressing, frightening or painful experiences, and even after the cause has been remedied, it may still take much time to regain his trust and confidence. In the case of a horse who has not previously displayed any signs of head-shyness, and who has not been mishandled, the handler might suspect a physical problem such as toothache, sinus or ear infection, and a vet should be consulted.

Care must obviously be exercised when bridling or grooming, offering and removing the bit gently and, if necessary, using a soft cloth rather than a brush when cleaning the head. Much time and patience will be needed to re-establish confidence, and at every opportunity the handler should attempt to handle the horse softly, stroking up the neck and as close to the head as possible, perhaps offering a titbit at the same time to encourage the horse to relax and lower his head. Resorting to brute force is not recommended, as it will only reinforce the horse's fears; coaxing and cajoling is to be preferred.

When handling the head, the horse should be untied – although he can be held by an assistant – in case he is frightened into pulling backwards. If he feels the restriction of being tied up, he will panic more, and the two memories will become associated (*see also* page 54).

Head Rubbing Against Handler

Nothing can be more painful than to receive a well-timed shove in the stomach from a horse's nose – particularly if he is wearing a lunge cavesson – or more irritating than to have a trail of slobbery green saliva wiped across clean clothes. There may be several causes:

1. The horse may be trying to relieve himself of discomfort caused by a badly fitting bit or bridle; in the case of a young horse, he may be trying to rid himself of the unaccustomed feel of the bit or bridle.

2. If the horse has just been worked, the sweaty areas on his face may cause him to rub against the nearest available surface, usually the handler.

3. The horse may be seeking attention, or perhaps demanding a titbit.

Tack should of course be checked for correct fit, and also joints of bits inspected for sharp, worn edges. Dried sweat should be gently brushed or rubbed off; in the summer the horse will probably appreciate having these areas wiped over with a damp sponge. Head rubbing is, nevertheless, a rather irritating habit which should be discouraged by firmly pushing the horse's head away with a sharp command 'No!'

Safety: Horses should never be left either tied up or standing loose in the stable with a bridle on because if he should try to rub his head to relieve an itch, he may dislodge the bridle and damage it. Worse still, if a bit ring becomes caught on a projection, such as a door bolt, the horse may well pull back in sudden panic, breaking the bridle, damaging the bit and probably injuring his mouth or neck muscles into the bargain.

Kicking

A horse who is known to kick should always be treated with a certain amount of caution, and children or novices kept at a distance from him. Most horses who kick do so as a means of defence: to get rid of, or protect themselves against, something which is seen as threatening or causing discomfort, such as a dog chasing him, the handler grooming sensitive areas roughly, or approaching the horse abruptly from the rear and startling him. A horse who is prone to kick is unlikely ever to be completely cured of the habit, although with the right sort of handling he may improve.

When approaching the horse, whether in the field or stable, the horse should be encouraged to come to the handler, by offering a titbit if necessary, and the head-collar put on straight away so that he is unable to swing his quarters around to present his back feet. While putting a head-collar on over the stable door is not normally advocated, it may be necessary to do so in extreme cases, or even to leave the headcollar on, although the dangers of this should be appreciated. When handling the horse in the stable, it is best to tie the horse up or to have an assistant hold him, so that he cannot corner the handler and kick.

Hitting the horse on the quarters is not advisable and, if anything, is more likely to cause the horse to kick out than to teach him a lesson, although a smack on the neck and a sharp reprimand may not be out of order. It should be remembered that this habit is often caused initially by bad treatment, and so any correction administered should be fair, and an effort made not to provoke the horse into kicking through thoughtless handling.

Fig 25 Avoid standing directly behind the horse. Grasp the end of the tail and exert a slight downwards pressure on it.

When performing tasks around the horse, such as grooming, it will help to have an assistant hold him, keeping his head turned slightly to the side on which the handler is standing. This will make it more difficult for the horse to kick out towards the handler. The assistant can also pick up one forefoot to help prevent the horse from kicking; it may not entirely prevent the horse if he is determined, but it will certainly limit his ability to do so.

When the handler is working in the immediate area of the quarters, he should try to avoid standing immediately behind the quarters, but stand to one side instead. The tailbone can be firmly grasped near its end in the free hand, and a slight downwards pressure exerted on it. This seems to have a slight inhibiting effect; just before the horse is about to kick, he will normally swish his tail violently and then clamp it down, so holding it will give the handler some warning of what is to follow. Standing close to the horse is safer than at a distance, so that if the horse does kick, he will push the handler away rather than injure him.

Horses who kick when in company should have a red ribbon plaited into the top of the tail hairs, and other riders warned not to crowd him. He should be kept to the edge of groups of other horses, and to the rear if in a ride. Those who kick when turned out in the field should be put in a paddock on their own, rather than risk injury to the others.

Leading Difficulties

Difficulties in leading tend to take two different forms: either the horse refuses to move altogether, or else does so with great reluctance, hanging back at each step (or, at the opposite extreme, the horse who is aware of his own strength and lacks discipline and obedience, may try to drag the handler off in whichever direction the horse wishes to go).

Ideally, horses should be taught to lead correctly while they are still foals: the youngster can be taught to wear a foal-slip or soft headcollar, and then encouraged to walk alongside the handler. Initially, the incentive to move forward can be provided by allowing the foal to walk alongside or behind his dam. As he gains more confidence, he can gradually be encouraged to walk at a short distance from his mother; if he starts to exhibit signs of reluctance to move forward, an arm placed behind his quarters to help push him forward is usually sufficient. On no account should the handler try to pull the foal forward by the headcollar, as this will only make him pull back again and struggle, and can result in problems later in life, not just when leading, but also when attempting to restrain him by tying him up.

Refusing to Move Forward / Walk Freely Beside Handler

This problem is usually fairly easy to remedy, although some assistance may be needed with more stubborn cases. The handler should put a bridle on the horse so as to exert more control, and carry a long schooling whip in the left hand. The horse should be firmly given the command 'Walk on!' and the handler can begin to move forward. Should the horse not follow suit, or move with extreme reluctance, he can be given a flick with the whip (used behind the handler's back) on his side. Some horses may take exception to this, hence the need for a bridle rather than a headcollar. Each time the horse starts to hang back, the command to walk should once more be given, if necessary reinforcing it with the whip.

More stubborn horses may need tougher tactics, in which case the assistant should stand behind him, out of kicking distance, with a stiff-bristled broom. If the horse disobeys or tries to pull backwards, and the whip does not produce the desired effect, the broom can be pushed firmly up against his quarters – most will immediately move forward with alacrity.

The handler should try to remain posi-

Fig 26 Leading correctly should be taught while the horse is still young.
Reluctance to move forward can usually be overcome by pushing him forward
from behind with one hand.

Fig 27 Pulling at the horse, getting in front of him, and staring at him will all encourage further resistance. (Photo: Mike Wood)

Fig 28 The same handler in a more sensible position beside the pony, and using a short stick to encourage him to move forwards. If a horse or pony reacts by swinging his quarters out sideways, the same method could be used but with a wall or hedge on the opposite side to the handler to keep him straight. Although horses are generally led from the near side, it can be useful in certain situations to teach him to lead correctly from both sides. (Photo: Mike Wood)

tioned between the horse's eye and shoulder, where he has most control and is in a relatively safe position. Allowing the horse to trail along behind is painful if the horse treads on the handler's heels, dangerous if he rears, and no real control can be exerted in an emergency. Getting in front of the horse's eye, or staring at him is also psychologically inhibiting, and will not encourage a free walk. Where the horse does not walk in a straight line, but continually wanders sideways, treading on the handler's feet, he can be encouraged to move at a small distance away by using the handle of the whip to give him a prod on the shoulder.

Rushing Forwards

At the opposite extreme, the horse who tries to rush off with the handler in tow can be a real problem, and should not be entrusted to a novice or child. If it only occurs at specific times, such as entering or leaving a stable, it may be due to more than just bad manners (see page 76). In addition to general bad manners and poor training, other causes may include the horse having been confined in his stable for overlong periods, or overfreshness.

The horse should be led in a bridle, which will give more control than a headcollar. When the horse attempts to make

Fig 29 Using a bridle when leading gives greater control than a headcollar. The handler should hold the reins behind the horse's jaw to prevent him from being able to bite the fingers.

Safety: The handler should wear gloves to protect the palms from injury should the horse attempt to pull away. Tying several knots along the length of a lead rope will also give a better grip. Lead ropes or reins should never be wrapped around the palm of the hand or wrist because, if the horse pulls away, they will tighten and, if it becomes really necessary, the handler will be unable to let go, which may result in broken bones. It is worth noting that the commonest of all horse-related injuries are those due to incorrect handling of lead ropes resulting in damage to the hands, sometimes even the loss of a thumb or finger.

If the horse is likely to be fractious, all gates leading out of the yard area to public roads should be closed.

a bid for freedom, he frequently does so by pushing his head to the right, away from the handler, before plunging forward. Keeping the horse's head and neck bent a little to the left will quite successfully prevent him from being able to break away in this manner – at most, all he will be able to do is circle around the handler, who should of course be careful to keep his feet out of the way.

If a little extra control is required, pushing the right elbow into the horse's neck will make it easier for the handler to keep him looking a little to the left and walking steadily.

Evasions When Lungeing

Lungeing is a useful exercise, but however carefully the horse is worked in this manner, at some point the handler may well have to deal with some kind of evasion or resistance. These are usually caused by confusion or lack of understanding on the part of the horse, by physical difficulties, or by bad organization and loss of initiative by the handler. Once the horse has learnt how to evade the handler in some way, it will require firm action and the handler must remain constantly alert to prevent

the horse from taking advantage of a moment's loss of concentration. Evasions and resistances can, of course, arise as a result of the horse becoming over-fatigued: lungeing is a strenuous and demanding exercise and for this reason should be limited to fifteen to twenty minutes' duration.

Horse Tries to Turn Inwards

Quite often, a horse will learn to turn inwards and will either halt, facing the handler, or will continue in the opposite direction (frequently because he is stiff and finds the work difficult). The handler must halt the horse and start him off on the lunge in the original direction again, (on a larger circle if the horse is finding it difficult to cope), this time paying strict attention to his positioning. The handler should stand so that he is opposite the horse's inside hip, so as to be able to drive the horse forward more effectively. Once the handler's position has deteriorated so as to become opposite the horse's eye, either because the horse has been allowed to become inactive or because the handler has edged sideways, it will have an inhibiting effect on the horse and the handler will no longer be in a position of authority.

Fig 30 Always use the correct equipment for the job: the horse is wearing a proper lunge cavesson, lunge rein, side reins (clipped up to the front of the saddle while the horse is inactive) and brushing boots all round. The handler is wearing sensible footwear, gloves and a hard hat, and carrying a lightweight, fibreglass lungeing whip. Note that the reins have been twisted around each other and looped through the bridle throatlash to prevent them from trailing on the ground (if it is not planned to ride the horse, they may be removed altogether). The stirrup irons have been run up the leathers, but are not properly secured; left like this they may work down and bang against the horse's sides.

Fig 31 Some horses can be very quick to seize the opportunity to turn inwards, especially if the handler loses his position of authority.

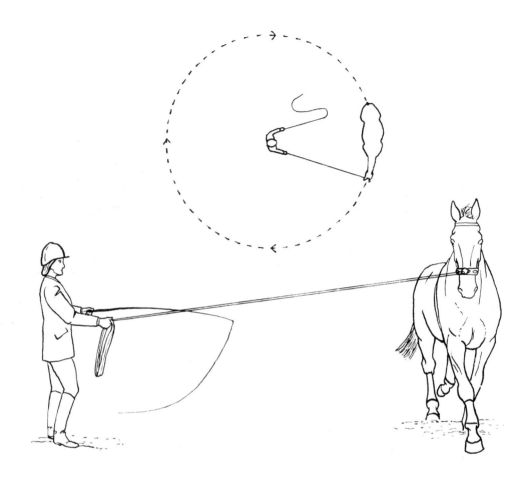

Fig 32 Maintaining a correct position in relation to the horse on the circle: the lunge rein and whip form a triangle, with the handler able to drive the horse forward effectively from a point opposite the horse's inside hip.

Some horses become very quick to seize the opportunity to turn inwards, and it may help to have an assistant hold the lunge rein at the centre of the circle, while the handler walks a smaller circle, allowing him to follow at a closer distance to the horse, carrying the whip to his rear, ready to forestall any tendency to whip round. This can also be a useful technique to use on a horse who tends to be idle.

If no assistance is available, the prob-lem can be dealt with by lungeing the horse in a saddle rather than a lunge roller. The outside stirrup iron can be run down the leather and secured to the girth with a spur strap or piece of twine, so that it does not bounce around. A second lunge rein is attached to the outside ring of the cavesson noseband, is passed through the stirrup iron and along the outside of the horse's body, around his quarters above the hocks, and back to the handler.

Fig 33 Lungeing using a second lunge rein to prevent the horse from turning inwards.

If the horse attempts to turn inwards, he can then be corrected by firm pressure on the second lunge rein. The handler should be competent at handling the equipment if he is to deal with the addition of a second lunge rein successfully, and some care should be taken initially as some horses will object at first to the feel of a lunge rein around the quarters.

Horse Does Not Obey Commands

This problem is usually caused by confusion, the horse not understanding what the handler requires of him. This lack of response to verbal commands may be because the horse has never before been taught them, or because the trainer uses unfamiliar commands, or fails to use the same commands each time. The best solution is to return to the basics, with an assistant leading the horse on the inside of the circle while the handler gives the commands. As the horse begins to associate the commands with the actions, so the assistant can gradually begin to move a short distance away from him until, finally, the assistant can be dispensed with altogether.

The handler should always repeat the commands for each gait in the same manner, rather than constantly changing either the words of the command, or the manner of delivery and inflexion. Generally, a short, sharp command with an upwards inflexion is most effective when asking for upwards transitions, while a soothing, lower-pitched tone using long drawn-out syllables – for example,

Horse Pulls Away From Handler

When using the whip, care should be taken not to flourish it in a manner that may frighten the horse, who may then attempt to put some distance between himself and the object of his fears. The whip should be used in a quiet manner, pointing the tip towards the inside rear fetlock, rather than raised, and flicked forwards towards the joint rather than cracked. The occasional flick of the whip actually touching the horse may occasionally be necessary, but it should not be used hard or as a means of punishment.

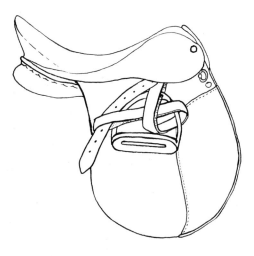

Fig 34 Stirrup irons correctly run up and secured when lungeing with a saddle.

'Wa-a- alk' – will help to slow or decrease the gait.

A common problem is when the horse is aware of what is required, but still refuses to slow down or halt when requested. If the horse is working in canter it is usually best to wait until the gait has wound down of its own accord to a trot or walk before attempting to do more. Circling the lunge rein in a backwards direction may help to slow the horse, but should be discontinued if the action agitates or upsets the horse. Failing this, the horse can be directed towards the nearest wall or hedge (which must be high enough to discourage the horse from attempting to jump it) and given the command 'Who-o-o-ah' as he comes face to face with it. The handler will need to position himself so that he is almost opposite the horse's inside eye as he does this so that the horse is unable to break past him. The handler can then approach and reward the horse.

Some horses can, however, be very strong on the lunge, particularly if they are very large and the handler on the short or light side. Rather than allow the horse to realize his full strength, it may be best to use a Wels pattern lunge cavesson which fits like a drop noseband and is effective although more severe and should be used with care. Alternatively, the lunge rein can be attached to the outside bit ring, run over the top of the poll, and threaded through the inside bit ring, passing back to the handler. This is also very effective, but severe, and changes the action of the bit to that of a gag.

> **Safety:** The handler should always wear gloves to protect the palms, and beware of wrapping the end of the lunge rein around the hand or wrist.

Shoeing Difficulties

Farriers cannot be blamed for refusing to shoe a horse who is difficult, but many

Fig 35 Farriers cannot be blamed for refusing to shoe a horse who is difficult, but sometimes the remedy lies in their own hands.

horses are often labelled as being such because of a bad experience in the past, such as a pricked sole, rough unsympathetic handling, or perhaps having been frightened by the noise (and smell in the case of hot shoeing). If the horse is young or stiff, or has a back or joint problem, he may also find the whole operation uncomfortable, particularly if the hind feet are held too high or pulled out too far to the side. Quite often the reason for a horse fidgeting is that he is uncomfortable, rather than actually frightened. If the farrier then becomes impatient and abrupt with such an 'uncooperative' horse, it is not surprising that eventually it becomes a real battle to get the shoes on and off

each time. Unfortunately, not all farriers are sympathetic towards a horse's problems or fears, and once you find a good farrier who is as skilful at handling horses as he is at shoeing them, it is worth sticking with him, even if he costs more than others in the area, or you have to travel the horse to him. (*See also* page 37.)

Youngsters can be prepared for shoeing by having their feet picked up and tapped with a light hammer, and it also helps if they can occasionally be stabled or placed in a field near to the shoeing area so they have a chance to get used to the sounds and smells. An older horse who has lost his confidence can have his apprehensions reduced a little by following the same procedure. With very difficult horses, a mild sedative may be advisable; it is not the most ideal solution, since the horse's co-ordination may be affected making it difficult for him to balance on three legs, and so veterinary advice should be sought first.

Tacking-Up Difficulties

Some horses are difficult to tack up and this can be because of discomfort, fear, or just reluctance to work. When tacking up, the handler should always try to be gentle: roughness will cause the horse to be awkward.

Saddle

The horse should first have a headcollar placed on him and he should be tied up, which will prevent him from wandering around the stable while the handler is trying to tack up. The saddle should be placed gently on the horse's back – not thumped down – and slightly forwards, towards the withers. It can then be slid back into the correct position, ensuring that all the hairs lie flat and in the right direction so they do not cause discomfort. If a numnah, or saddle cloth, is used, it should be pulled well up into the front arch of the saddle, so that it does not press down upon the withers and rub.

Fig 36 Each foreleg in turn can be drawn forward to smooth out any wrinkles of skin beneath the girth.

The girth should be gently lowered down – not thrown over, when the buckles will inevitably bang against the horse's knees, making him fidget. It should be tightened firmly but not abruptly, and each foreleg drawn forward in turn to smooth out the skin creases behind the elbows so as to prevent pinching.

Saddles should fit correctly, and regular checks made as the horse may change shape over the year according to fitness, and the amount of work and food he is receiving. Should the horse suddenly become difficult about having the saddle put on, then, not only fit, but damage such as a broken tree should be checked for. The back should also be inspected for signs of injury which may be causing discomfort; this can be caused by a rider who sits awkwardly, and not necessarily by the saddle. Sores and rub marks are usually immediately obvious, but sometimes tenderness is apparent to the touch, if not visible to the eye. Girths should not be so wide or so narrow that they actually cut into the horse's skin.

Bridle

Many horses can also be difficult to bridle, especially when the horse is large and the handler short. This often happens through having his head roughly handled, and particularly if he has his teeth painfully banged with the bit either when putting the bridle on or taking it off. If the horse puts his head up in the air out of the reach of the handler, the reins can be unbuckled, placed around the neck and then fastened again, to give the handler something to hold if the horse tries to wander off. The loop of the headpiece can be used to capture the end of the nose and

Fig 37 Bringing the right arm around the front of the horse's face will stop him from being able to raise his head impossibly high while being bridled.

draw it downwards, when the handler can then bring one arm around the front of his face to prevent him from raising his head out of reach again. The bridle cheekpieces can then be held in the hand of this restraining arm while the free hand offers the bit.

Some horses will resolutely refuse to open their mouths to take the bit, but the handler can overcome this by inserting the thumb of the hand supporting the bit into the corner of the horse's mouth where there is a gap between front and back teeth, and pressing down on the tongue.

Offering a titbit in the palm of the hand at the same time, or smearing the mouthpiece with something tasty such as treacle or even a little toothpaste, will soon make it a pleasurable experience for the horse. When removing the bit, the mouthpiece should once again be supported with the fingers to help guide it out, so that it does not bang against the front teeth. If the horse is reluctant to let go of the bit or is headshy and likely to pull away abruptly, a titbit can be offered.

The handler should make sure that the noseband (and curb chain, if used) is undone before removing the bridle because, if left fastened, it will make it difficult to remove the bit gently. (*See* page 39.)

Difficulty in Tying Up

Horses should never be left tied up and unattended; inevitably, it is always when the handler's back is turned that accidents happen. Should something startle the horse and he jumps backwards in surprise, the feeling of restraint and being trapped may cause him to panic and struggle violently until eventually something snaps – the lead rope, headcollar or possibly the horse's neck. At best, he may be left loose and looking for escape; more seriously he may fall over in his struggle and injure himself – damage to the neck musculature or spinal column may be sustained. Whatever the outcome, the horse will certainly be difficult to tie up safely in the future, particularly if he has frightened himself. Less anxious types will have learnt that they can free themselves again in the future whenever they do not wish to be tied up. Even if this is the case, the horse should nevertheless always be tied

Fig 38 Quick release knot.

to a loop of string which will break under stress, rather than directly to a fixed ring. A quick-release knot should also be used so that if the horse should panic for some reason, the handler can quickly untie and soothe him; most horses will settle again once the feeling of restriction is relaxed. The horse should never be tied up using the reins of the bridle because if he pulls back, the bit can do a considerable amount of damage to the mouth.

If the horse does begin to show signs of panic at being tied up, tugging at the rope to try and pull the horse forward will only make the matter worse. The horse should have the tension on the lead rope relaxed and then be pushed forward by a hand on the quarters again. If the horse appears to be genuinely anxious, the handler should also speak soothingly to the horse, and try to reassure him. Once the horse is relaxed again, he can be tied up once more, perhaps with a little more slack in the rope, and with a haynet to nibble at.

If the horse has learnt to pull back purposely in order to free himself (rather than to escape a sense of restriction), the handler can attempt to teach him to stand quietly in one of two ways:

1. An assistant can stand just behind the horse with a stiff-bristled yard broom, and when the horse starts to hang backwards, push the bristles firmly against his quarters to encourage him to move forward again. This should not be done with an easily frightened, or nervous horse.

2. The handler can attach a long line, such as a lunge rein, to a headcollar, loop it through a ring on the wall, and keep hold of the end while working around the horse. As the horse begins to pull backwards the line can be played out so there is no direct pressure for him to lean against. The horse can then be led forward again, the slack taken up once more, and given the command to 'Stand'. This

Fig 39 Using a long lunge line looped through a ring in the wall with a horse who is difficult to tie up.

method can also be useful when dealing with a nervous horse although, easiest of all, is to ask an assistant to hold the horse, rather than tie him up.

Some experts advocate various methods using ropes fixed in various ways to teach the horse to stand while tied up, but these systems are probably better left to the experts as some can be potentially injurious. It is, however, well worth taking the time to teach the horse to stand on command, as it can be useful in many situations when riding or mounting as well as when tying him up.

Difficulty in Trimming Up

Not surprisingly, many horses find mane- and tail-pulling a painful process, and care should be taken as regards both the handler's safety and the horse's comfort. When pulling the mane or tail, only a few hairs at a time should be removed, wrapping them once or twice around a comb, as near to the roots as possible and then jerking them out quickly. This is easiest to do whilst the horse is still warm after exercise, and if a little is done each day a neat appearance will soon be achieved and is easily maintained. It is best not to have a

Fig 40 Mane pulling should be done in easy stages so as not to make the horse sore.

major tidying-up session, as this will leave the horse feeling sore and inclined to rub, and he will be less co-operative about the matter next time.

Some horses seem to object violently to having the mane pulled with a comb', but less so if just the fingertips are used. Wearing a plastic washing-up glove or rubber thimbles will protect the fingers from soreness and give a better purchase on the hairs.

When pulling tails, the handler is obviously at risk from a kick and if the horse is likely to prove fractious it may be a wise precaution to have an assistant hold the horse inside a stable, with his tail hanging over the bottom door. A blanket or similar placed over the door first will prevent damage to the underside of the tail where the skin is sensitive. If the horse really objects strenuously to having his mane and tail pulled, a reasonably neat effect can be achieved by using a razor comb, which can be bought from a chemist.

Consideration should, of course, always be given to the horse's lifestyle when tidying up his appearance. If he has to live out for all or much of the time, it is kindest to leave the forelock fairly long and the tail untouched so as to provide some degree of protection against flies in summer, and also against windy, wet weather in the winter. When a smart appearance is required, a plaited tail is more troublesome and time-consuming than a pulled one, but looks equally as attractive.

Another area often trimmed and which can cause problems is the whiskers on the horse's muzzle. It is mainly a matter of

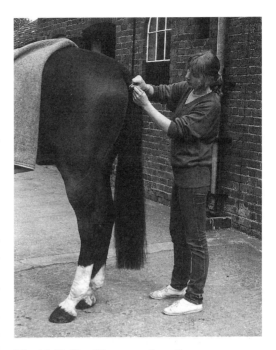

Fig 41 Tail pulling can place the handler in a hazardous position and fractious horses might be more safely dealt with over the stable door.

personal preference as to whether these are left or removed, but it is worth remembering that they do function as sensory organs and many horses will find it irritating when the handler tries to cut them off. A plastic disposable safety razor is probably the quickest, safest and neatest way of removing the whiskers, but if the horse really objects violently to having them removed, it is best to leave them rather than persist.

Horses who fidget when having the feathers trimmed up can be easily dealt with by lifting the foot opposite to the leg which the handler is working on.

CHAPTER 3

In the Stable

A large number of vices and problems are associated with stabled horses. The handler should bear in mind that being confined in a small area – often for long hours with little or no stimulation – is not a natural way of life for a horse.

Whenever possible, the horse should be allowed out at grass each day, the longer the better, and preferably with other (friendly) company of his own kind. Even a few hours is better than nothing, and if the horse's food intake has to be strictly controlled for some reason, then a bare paddock is still a better alternative than keeping him cooped up all the time.

When it is necessary for the horse to be stabled, he should be provided with a haynet to keep him occupied. Some horses are greedy, and quickly wolf down their allotted ration, and if it has to be restricted the problem can to a degree be overcome by using a haynet with small holes. This will force the horse to spend more time in teasing out the stalks of hay and will slow down the process of consumption. Another useful idea is to buy a large swede or turnip and drill a hole through the centre of it. A piece of rope or plaited baler twine can then be threaded through the hole and the turnip suspended in the stable, perhaps by the doorway. This simple device can provide hours of entertainment, giving the horse something to nibble at, but which he is unable to get a really good grasp on with his teeth so he is unable to devour the lot within a few bites. While on the subject of 'toys', some horses do appreciate being given some kind of plaything, such as a football in the stable, or a stout rubber ring of the type sold as toys for dogs in pet shops and which can be hung in the stable doorway with a piece of plaited baler twine.

Consideration should be given to the position of the horse's stable within the yard, not just from the point of view of physical well-being, but with his psychological contentment in mind, too. This will to a large extent be dictated by the handler's knowledge of the horse's temperament and personality. More outgoing types who become easily bored will enjoy being able to see out over their doors and watching any activity going on in the yard. More nervous or easily startled horses will probably do better in a quieter location with fewer disturbances. Stabling the horse next to one whom he does not get on with can be very stressful, and is hardly conducive to producing a relaxed, contented individual. Adopting the attitude that the horse will just have to learn to live with things as they are is a negative attitude; matters are unlikely to improve, and the chances are that the horse never will learn to get used to it.

Horses also prefer a regular routine, and one should be established and adhered to as strictly as possible. Irregular feed times especially can lead not only to digestive disturbances, but can prove very distressing for some animals, who begin to fret and actually worry weight off.

Altogether far too many horses suffer from overfeeding, overconfinement and a lack of exercise, and this can be the source of many problems, both in the stable, while being handled and under saddle.

Bedding

Bed Eating

Bed eating is an undesirable habit, not only because it removes the handler's control over feed intakc, but, more importantly, for reasons of physical health: bed eating can lead to digestive problems such as colic, and aggravate respiratory diseases.

A horse who eats his bedding may be doing so from boredom (in a natural state he would be grazing for much of the day) and because of a lack of roughage in his diet, particularly if he is on a high concentrate ration, with a consequently reduced amount of hay. In the latter instance, the hay ration should never be reduced to less than 25 per cent of the total daily food intake; roughage is essential for the correct digestion of food, as much as to satisfy the horse's natural craving for bulk.

In some cases, it may be noted that the horse is eating his bedding in preference to hay which has been provided for him, in which case, the forage should be checked for its quality and palatability. Clean, straw bedding will be much more desirable to him than musty hay. The horse may perhaps have been switched to haylage, which can have an off-putting taste

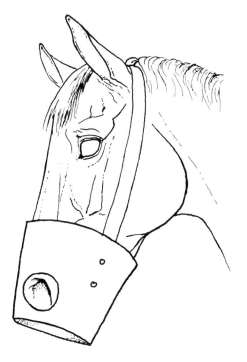

Fig 42 A 'Bucket' muzzle, not the most ideal solution to bed (or dung) eating, but a last resort. The cause should be sought and remedied, rather than merely treating the symptoms.

and smell to an animal not accustomed to it. The haylage should be introduced slowly, mixing it thoroughly with a proportion of hay to start with, gradually increasing the quantity as the horse becomes used to it.

If the horse wolfs down his ration of hay, and then turns his attention to the straw bed, using a haynet with smaller holes will help to slow him down, keeping him occupied for longer. When adding fresh bedding, mix the new in thoroughly with the older, soiled straw so as to make it less palatable and harder to pick out; this will also create a better, springier bed. In addition, a weak solution of disinfectant and water may be sprinkled over the surface of the newly laid bed to discourage eating.

If these measures fail, the only other solution is to turn to an inedible form of bedding such as woodshavings or shredded paper. If the horse persists in attempting to eat such bedding, veterinary advice should be sought, as it may be a sign of a severe digestive disorder.

Scraping Up Bedding

There may be several reasons for a horse

Fig 43 Adequate forage should be allowed the horse, particularly if he is stabled for long periods of time. Note the potential hazard of the bucket holder on the floor of the stable.

disturbing his bedding including: feeling cold, discomfort (perhaps caused by slipping rugs), strange surroundings and restlessness caused by insufficient exercise. If the horse does not normally make a habit of scraping up his bedding, it may be assumed that disturbed bedding is a sign that the horse has suffered (or is suffering) a bout of colic. If scrape marks are also visible on the walls,he may have become cast (*see* page 64). Horses who are bored may dig up their bedding, as might those who have been changed on to a different and unfamiliar bedding, although in the latter case the habit usually stops with time.

If the bedding is regularly scraped up, the handler should ensure that sufficient exercise is given, plus some freedom in a turnout paddock each day. Adequate forage should be provided, as the pawing action may be related to searching for food (horses in a field on a snowy day can be observed to do this in order to uncover the grass beneath). There is a danger that if a considerable amount of bedding is scraped up exposing bare areas of flooring, the horse may injure himself when he lies down. Placing thick rubber mats on the floor beneath the bed will help provide some protection against this happening.

Do note the horse's stance while he is in the stable. If he consistently scrapes up his bedding to form a pile which he then stands upon, with either his quarters or front limbs higher, he may be attempting to relieve some kind of physical discomfort by forming a gradient. If this is the case, consult your vet.

Bolting Feed

A horse who gulps down his food quickly is

not behaving either in a natural manner or in one calculated to help him make the most of his concentrate ration. Food which is eaten over-hastily will not be properly masticated or mixed with saliva, and can lead to choking, digestive disorders and unthriftiness.

Try to isolate the cause of the problem in order to find the most satisfactory solution:

1. Great hunger. In the natural state, the horse would normally be grazing for much of the time, and his gut would never be entirely empty. Under artificial, stabled conditions, mealtimes are infrequent in comparison with the natural, almost continuous, grazing habit, and especially so if the diet has to be restricted for some reason such as obesity, or because the horse is competing and a full, distended stomach would interfere with the efficient functioning of the respiratory system.

Giving a small haynet before a short feed will help take the edge off his appetite and will also encourage the secretion of gastric juices so that the concentrate feed which follows will be digested more efficiently. Adding some chaff to the feed will encourage the horse to chew each mouthful more carefully before swallowing it. Large chunks of rock salt placed in the feed manger or bucket may also slow down eating by forcing the horse to pick around them.

2. The horse may feel threatened by the presence of either another horse or horses, or a human. If he thinks his food is going to be stolen from him, he will simply attempt to eat as much as possible as quickly as he can. Try to ensure that he is left alone in peace and quiet at meal

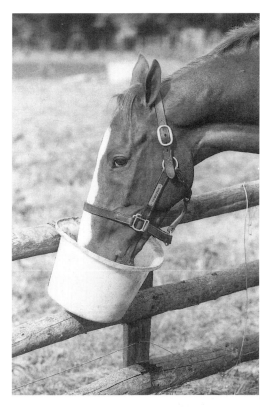

Fig 44 Even the presence of a human being can disturb the horse or make him feel threatened while he is eating.

times, rather than bothering him by trying to groom or muck out at the same time. If he is fed in a field with several horses, remove him and feed him away from the others so he feels secure and will not be subject to bullying.

3. Haphazard routines soon make horses anxious and irritable. Try to stick to regular feed times as far as possible, so the horse does not fret and is less likely to bolt his feed when it does finally arrive.

Fig 45 Too close a contact between horses who do not get on with each other
can be immensely stressful for some individuals.

Box Walking

A horse who 'box walks' – or paces round and round his stable – is one who is unhappy with his situation. It can be a reaction to being kept close to another horse he does not get on with, or simply that he cannot tolerate being kept in close confinement. Horses who fall into the latter category are probably better off being kept out at grass instead, with a field shelter. If this is not feasible, he should certainly be turned out as much as possible, and preferably with company of his own kind.

The yard routine might also be examined: if there is little going on outside the stable, or he is kept in an area where he cannot see a great deal of what is going on, he may be bored and, lacking in company or other stimulus, try to distract himself in any way possible. It can also be a nervous habit, in which case a slightly different method of management might be called for, where a regular routine without an excessive amount of noise, bustle and general activity going on outside might be preferable. It is a case of studying the animal's reactions to the current environment.

Some authorities advise putting bales of straw in the way, or hanging rubber tyres from the ceiling, but while these measures may make it more difficult for the horse to box walk, it will not prevent him. Tying the horse up is impractical and it is unfair to leave the horse tied up for long periods anyway, not to mention dangerous if he attempts to lie down. A long rope with a sinker is more humane, but still denies the horse a great deal of mobility, and does little to deal with the root cause of the problem, which may result in his adopting another vice instead.

Knocking Over Buckets

Some horses will habitually knock their water buckets over when in the stable, which results in sodden bedding, and if it happens late at night, the horse may be deprived of water for a lengthy period as a result. The habit may be caused by bad placement of the water bucket – if it is too close to a doorway and the horse spends much time looking out into the yard, for example, it may be knocked over. It may also be because of boredom, the horse playing with the bucket simply because he has nothing much else to do.

The most obvious solution to the problem is to remove the necessity for a water bucket altogether, replacing it with an automatic watering system. However, this may not be practical for one reason or another, and some horses will play with the water instead, still managing to soak a considerable portion of the bedding. Another alternative, which is considerably cheaper, is to obtain an old car tyre and place the filled bucket in the centre. The problem is that once the bucket is nearly, or completely empty, the horse can easily remove it with his teeth and throw it across the stable, resulting in damage to the bucket and risking injury to the horse.

Fig 46 A bucket holder made from an old tyre. Handles should preferably be removed in case a foot becomes trapped in it.

Probably the most satisfactory option is to invest in a large plastic dustbin. When three-quarters full of water it is too heavy for the horse to kick or knock over, and the large volume of water makes it unlikely that the horse will drink enough to make it light enough to move. Provided the dustbin is not filled right to the brim, the water level will be sufficiently low to prevent the horse from thoroughly soaking his bedding even if he does play with it.

In the case of the horse who kicks his feed bucket over, the cause is most likely to be impatience, especially if chaff or pieces of rock salt have been added to prevent the horse from bolting his feed. Much of the feed will then end up being trampled into the ground with the front feet and wasted. A fixed manger, or else one of the portable types which can be hung over the top of a door can be used instead, and feeding should be kept to a regular time as far as possible to prevent him from becoming irritable.

Cast

A horse is said to be cast when he is lying so close to a wall that he traps his front legs and is unable to rise without assistance. This may happen if a stable is too small, or if the horse attempts to roll, and actually turns right over, bringing him too close to an adjacent wall. Some horses seem to get cast frequently, which can be a cause of great worry to the owner, since although some will lie quietly until help arrives, others will panic and thrash frantically around, damaging the stable and their legs in the process.

On finding a cast horse, the handler should summon additional help from another person. If the bedding has become scraped up, more should be placed in the stable so that the horse does not injure himself further. To prevent further struggling and abortive efforts to rise, the horse should be immobilized temporarily by kneeling on the neck just behind the cheekbone. Once the horse is quiet, two lunge lines will be needed, one placed around a foreleg, the other around a hind leg, above the knee and hock joints. Each person then takes the end of one line, and the horse can be rolled over onto his other side. The horse will probably scramble to his feet immediately, and the handlers should take care not to be in the way of his feet as he does so. If the animal has been cast for some time and has been struggling, he may well be exhausted from his efforts.

The cause for the horse becoming cast should be investigated, with a view to preventing it from happening again. These may include:

1. The horse, having been returned to his box covered with sweat, rolls to try and make himself feel more comfortable. Many horses enjoy a roll after exercise, anyway, even if they have been properly

cooled down and brushed off afterwards, and it may help to take the horse to an area where he can have a good roll if he feels inclined.

2. The horse may have suffered (or be suffering) a bout of colic, the pain of which has caused him to roll in an attempt to relieve the discomfort. Veterinary advice should be sought, and the cause of the colic investigated and remedied.

3. The stable may be too small.

4. The stable may be too large for the size of the horse, and the sense of space may encourage him to roll right over.

Horizontal slats of wood can be fastened to the interior of the kicking boards, which will give the horse's hooves some purchase

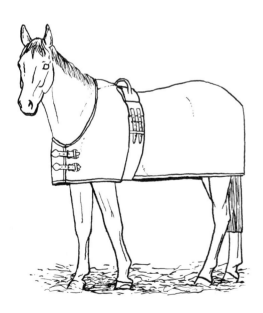

Fig 47 Anti-cast roller.

in the event of his becoming cast again, thus enabling him to push himself away from the wall. An anti-cast roller which has a large metal hoop inserted where it passes over the spine will also help to discourage the horse from attempts to roll right over. If the horse does succeed in becoming cast in such a roller (and it has happened before) the roller should be removed or cut off before attempting to help roll the horse over the other way.

Claustrophobia

As with people, horses can suffer from claustrophobia, a fear of being confined in an enclosed space. Horses thus affected will show signs of fear and panic: wide, staring eyes, tenseness, and possibly sweating. Those who are only mildly affected may be able to tolerate stabling for short periods – overnight, for example – provided the stable is large and airy, preferably with a high ceiling, and a view to the outside. More profoundly affected horses may refuse to enter a confined space at all, even under considerable duress. There is no point in forcing the horse: horses are unable to rationalize and come to terms with their fears in the same way as humans can, and to persist will only increase the animal's distress and is not far short of cruelty. It is quite possible to keep a horse out at grass all the year round, if a little less convenient for the handler.

Crib Biting

Once a horse has become confirmed in the habit of crib biting, it is virtually impos-

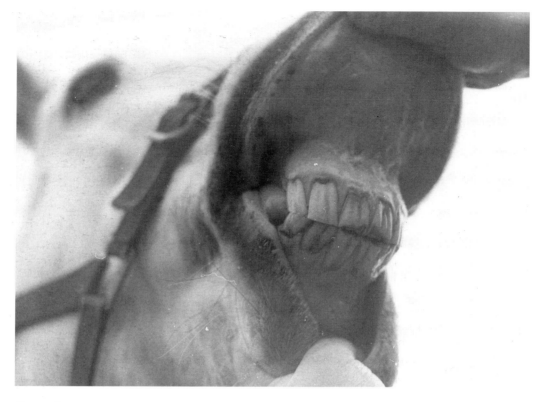

Fig 48 Damage to the front teeth often results from crib biting.

sible to prevent it, even with a change of diet, environment and management. Boredom, lack of activity, stress and lack of forage may all be contributory causes of this vice, and in some cases youngsters may imitate a horse who crib bites if he observes the habit regularly. It is certainly worth bearing in mind, though, that it is not a habit which horses indulge in when living in the wild, but is purely associated with those kept in the largely unnatural environments which we provide for them.

The horse will grasp any available projection – the top of a stable door, any convenient ledges or the tops of the kicking boards within the stable – with his front teeth and, arching his neck, will swallow air, making a peculiar and unpleasant gulping sound as he does so. The consequent presence of air in the stomach can lead to digestive disorders and may be responsible for recurrent attacks of colic as well as being responsible for poor digestion, so animals prone to this vice may be poor doers. Damage will also be caused to the front teeth, which will become chipped and unevenly worn so that grazing efficiency may eventually become impaired.

Prevention is the best policy, and the handler should ensure that the horse is not left standing in a stable for long periods with nothing to occupy him. It is natural for horses to spend much of their time grazing, and it is possible that crib biting may be a response to this urge to graze. Grasping a projection with the front teeth imitates biting off grass stems, while swallowing air distends the stomach as grazed forage would do normally. When it is necessary for the horse to be stabled, he should, if possible, be given a haynet.

Once the horse has actually acquired the habit of crib biting, prevention can be effected either through use of a crib strap, which physically stops the horse from being able to swallow air when his neck is arched, or by means of surgery which often has only limited success.

Turning the horse out to grass whenever possible may help to distract him temporarily, but the vice is likely to return when the horse is put back in the stable. Even so, the horse may still crib bite even when out at grass, using fences and gates.

Projections within the stable which the horse can use to crib bite should be kept to a minimum, feed buckets being used instead of fixed mangers which cannot be removed when not in use, and the kicking boards should reach from floor to ceiling. The tops of doors should have a metal strip attached to limit the damage which may be done to them, and any wooden surfaces showing the tell-tale evidence of teeth marks should have a coat of creosote applied – to preserve the wood as much as to make it taste bitter. Applying a proprietary brand of unpleasant-tasting preparation to projection surfaces may discourage the horse from grasping them with his teeth, but can be a little messy, and the animal may simply learn to windsuck instead (*see* page 82).

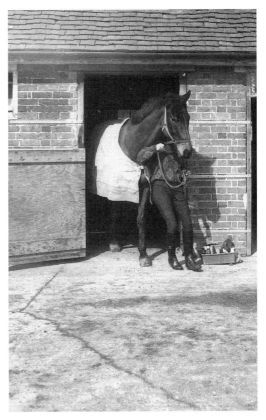

Fig 49 Barging out of (or into) a stable is a hazard not just to the horse, but to the handler as well.

Doors

Door Barging

A horse who barges into, or out of, his stable is a hazard not just to himself, but to his handler who may be crushed against a door jamb or knocked over; it can certainly be an alarming experience for a novice or nervous person.

Rushing into or out of the stable may be due either to fear or just plain bad manners – the horse may be anxious to manners get to his feed for example – and the handler will need to determine which is the cause before deciding upon the best course of action to take:

1. Fear. The horse may be afraid of being hurt; perhaps in the past a stable door has blown shut on him, or he has banged his head on a low door frame. For this reason, whenever leading a horse in or out of a door or gateway, care should be taken to ensure first that doors are fully opened and wedged if necessary to prevent gusts of wind from blowing them back again. Stable doorways should also be wide and high enough for both horse and handler to move through in comfort and safety. A minimum width should be 4ft 6in (1.4m) and minimum height 7ft (2.1m). Leading the horse through the opening in a straight line, rather than at an angle, will also reduce the danger of a hip being caught.

A horse who is anxious about catching his head can be offered a titbit of a little food in a bucket to encourage him to lower his head as he walks through the doorway.

The handler should be ready for the horse to try and rush forward and if he attempts to do so, a firm contact should be taken on the lead rope or reins, and a firm but soothing command such as 'Steady' given. Shouting at the horse is more likely to alarm him further. Praise him when there is any sign of improvement.

In some cases, the horse may actually panic more if he feels he is being crowded by the handler as he moves through the doorway, and regardless of any actions the handler may take, will persist in pushing him aside and rushing headlong into the box. In such instances, it is sometimes safer for all concerned not to be too insistent: the horse should be led to the entrance of the doorway and allowed to progress through it on his own and at his own rate.

If the horse is leaving his stable in this manner, there should be another person stationed just outside the doorway to catch hold of him as he emerges.

2. Bad manners. If barging is due to bad manners, try not to exacerbate the situation by leaving feeds, haynets, etc. in the stable which will only make the horse (particularly if he is greedy) more anxious to enter quickly. A horse who pushes his handler to one side when entering or leaving a stable is demonstrating a lack of respect for the handler's authority. When generally handling the horse, always insist that he moves across, rather than pushes against the handler, to try and instil a sense of the latter's dominance and superiority. When leading in or out of the stable, use a bridle or lunge cavesson which will provide more control than a headcollar and lead rope, and carry a short stick. Assume that the horse is going to behave, but do not be complacent!

Safety: Do wear gloves to protect the hands. Do not jerk at the lead rope or reins as it is most likely to frighten the horse into throwing his head upwards and banging it on the lintel. When opening stable doors, undo the bottom bolt first, and then the top one. If the horse attempts to barge out (or even if he is only leaning against the door) you will be in a better position to deal with it, and are less likely to be knocked unconscious!

Fig 50 A breast bar. (Photo: Mike Wood)

As soon as the horse makes any attempt to dive forward, sharply reprimand him with your voice and, if necessary, smack him once, sharply, across the chest with the stick.

In order to make completing stable chores easier, and to enable the handler to enter or leave the stable without the horse pushing past each time he sees even the merest crack appearing as the door opens, it is well worth going to the extra effort and expense of having a breast bar fitted (*see* page 70).

Door Climbing

Some horses just cannot cope with confinement, however well appointed and spacious the stable, and will attempt to escape by climbing or jumping over the bottom door, even if the space is obviously too small for them to do so. It can be prevented by fitting a metal grille or closing the top door, but the latter practice will certainly interfere with the circulation of fresh air and will only add to the feeling of confinement and isolation from the outside world; the horse may panic and actually throw himself around in the box, injuring himself in the process and making it dangerous for anyone to approach him. This is related to claustrophobia (*see* page 65) and the handler may have to resign himself to keeping the horse out at grass. It may be possible to reach some kind of compromise by keeping the horse in either a large barn or an open yard with a shelter available, preferably with company.

Sometimes a horse may attempt to climb out over the lower door not because he is claustrophobic, but out of excitement: perhaps because he is in a strange yard, because it is feed time, or a particular companion is going out and leaving him behind. In these circumstances, the handler should join the horse in the stable to provide reassurance and to restrain him; a headcollar or bridle should be put on him to provide some means of control. If this is not possible for some reason, then shutting the top door or fitting a metal grille would seem a reasonable action since it is only a temporary measure for a short period of time.

Door Kicking

Kicking at stable doors can be highly irritating for people in the near vicinity, as well as damaging to the stable door and surrounding woodwork. Quite often the habit may start as a result of poor management, and the horse vents his frustration in one of the few ways available to him.

If allowed to continue unchecked, this can lead to physical problems such as bruised and possibly permanently enlarged knee and fetlock joints, and jarred feet – in extreme cases it can lead to lameness. The problem should be dealt with considering both immediate prevention and a longer-term solution:

1. Remove the cause as far as possible. During the daytime in dry, warm weather, a breast bar fitted across the doorway will eliminate the need for a bottom door altogether, although this is obviously not very practical during the winter months. Shutting the top door or fitting a grille so that the horse cannot get close enough to the lower door to kick it is less satisfactory, as the horse may simply retreat to the back of the box and develop some other equally irritating stable vice, or use his back feet against a rear wall.

Padding the interior of the door in some manner is preferable and although it will not actually prevent the horse from kicking, it will at least reduce the danger of injury and, to a degree, will muffle the noise.

2. Door kicking is largely an expression of frustration. It is not a natural state of affairs for a horse to spend long periods of time in close confinement, and some tolerate it less well than others. The animal should be turned out to grass as much as possible and, when stabled, a regular supply of hay should be provided to try and eliminate boredom; the horse should also receive sufficient exercise. A turnip might also be provided, suspended from a length of rope: nibbling at this will give the horse a little entertainment as well as a little variety in the diet.

3. Door kicking can also be a means of attracting attention, as much as a means of expressing psychological frustration. If the horse is more inclined to kick the door at certain times, take note of the fact, and consider whether the stable routine might be adjusted in some way to deal with this. If the horse kicks the door mainly at feed times, for example, he is plainly demanding to be fed, so feed him first as making him wait will not teach him anything, but merely create even more irritation and stress.

Door Opening

Escape artists in the shape of horses who have learned, either by imitating others, or by accident, how to undo their stable door bolts, are not uncommon. It can be a real problem, as a horse who lets himself out places himself and passers-by at risk, especially if the stables are close to the road. Once the trick has been learnt, it is almost impossible to try and cure it, and, instead, the handler can only take measures to stop the horse from being successful in his attempts.

A bottom bolt should be fitted to the lower door, preferably a proper stable bolt which has a curved piece of metal at the end which hooks around a protruding piece of metal with a hole in it. A spring- or trigger-clip from a lead rope can then be clipped through the hole when the bolt is pushed home. This will prevent the horse from working the lower bolt back by the simple expedient of kicking at the door.

Kick bolts, whilst convenient for the handler, can also be dislodged in this manner, and so are not effective in keeping a determined horse in.

A padlock should not be placed on the top bolt, as it is too hazardous in the case of an outbreak of fire, when it may be essential to release the horse quickly. Neither is it a good policy to place a spring- or trigger-clip on the top bolt to stop the horse from drawing it back. The horse will soon learn to manipulate it and remove it from the door; and there have also been many instances of horses receiving nasty injuries caused by the hook part of a spring-clip penetrating the lips. A better solution is to fit a proper 'horse-proof' bolt, which is a completely enclosed mechanism that the horse is unable to open.

Refusal to Drink

Horses should preferably have a supply of fresh water available to them at all times in the stable; it is essential to the correct functioning of the body systems. The daily water intake varies from one individual to the next, but is generally higher in summer than in winter. There are occasions, however, when a horse will refuse to drink, which if allowed to continue will lead to dehydration. There are many possible causes of a horse refusing to drink:

Fig 51 Daily water intake varies from one horse to another, but fresh water should be available at all times, whether in the field or stable.

1. Ill health. Other symptoms will probably also be present, and a vet should be consulted. Where blockage-type colics are involved, the horse may show a marked reluctance to drink, washing his mouth out rather than actually swallowing any of the liquid.

2. Type of water container. An unfamiliar container may be off-putting, as may an automatic waterer. Some horses never come to terms with the latter, and have to be given a bucket.

3. Taste. The water of a new environment the horse has been moved to may smell or taste different from that which he is used to. With time and familiarity, the horse will drink, and can be encouraged to do so initially by adding something the horse likes, such as the water which sugar beet has been soaked in. Water given in buckets should be changed at least twice a day, regardless of whether the horse has finished it, or whether it still appears to be relatively clean. The practice of topping up a half-emptied bucket should be discouraged. Water standing in a stable tends to absorb ammonia from the atmosphere and will develop a stale taste repellent to more fastidious horses.

4. Excitement. An excited horse may refuse to drink, but once he has settled down and relaxed, will do so.

5. Exhaustion. A horse who is very tired may be reluctant to drink, even if he is dehydrated. Once he has had time to recover (a double handful of glucose added to the feed can do wonders to perk a tired horse up a little) he should start to drink again. If an electrolyte solution has been added to the water bucket to help with the recovery rate, and he is unused to such substances, it could possibly be the cause of his reluctance to drink. If the horse still refuses water after he has had time to recover from his labours, a vet should be consulted.

6. Contamination. Horses have a sensitive sense of taste and smell, and contamination of the water can lead the horse to refuse to drink. Droppings, hay, feed or bedding which have fallen into the bucket can make it objectionable to the horse. If the bucket has been disinfected, the smell can linger and be off-putting: if it is necessary to disinfect it, use one of the solutions which are sold in chemists for sterilizing babies' bottles. Buckets should also be situated in an area where the horse is least likely to foul it with his droppings, or by dropping food into it.

Eating Droppings (Coprophagia)

In certain circumstances, eating his own droppings is not the unnatural practice it appears, although it is certainly an unpleasant one from the handler's point of view. A young foal might eat his droppings as a means of building up his own gut bacteria, or a horse treated with antibiotics may do so for similar reasons if his gut bacteria have become depleted as a result of the treatment.

Eating droppings for any other reason, however, denotes extreme hunger, a dietary deficiency of some kind, or possibly boredom. It is generally not desirable from the point of view of worm re-infestation. The droppings should be frequently removed from the stable, and a supply of hay provided to occupy the horse's attention. A general mineral and vitamin supplement can be added to the feed, but if this does not improve the situation, veterinary advice should be sought. The horse should also be allowed sufficient freedom at grass, rather than being left standing in the stable where he will become bored.

Refusal to Eat

There may be a number of reasons for a horse refusing to eat his concentrate feed, including some of those for his not drinking (see page 71). In addition to ill health, dislike of the feed container, excitement and exhaustion, other causes may be:

1. Sore mouth or sharp teeth. This problem may need veterinary attention – for example, the teeth may need rasping. The horse may be seen to quid while eating, that is to say, drop pieces of partially chewed food out of the side of his mouth. Until the cause of the problem has been corrected, the horse should be given soft, easily chewed foods, and his hay softened by placing it in a dustbin and pouring boiling water over it. A lid can be fitted over the top so that the steam does not escape, and the hay given to the horse once it has cooled.

2. Different foodstuff. A good horse manager will never make an abrupt change to the horse's concentrate ration, but will introduce new foodstuffs gradually so as to avoid causing digestive upsets. Even a change of brand rather than type of food (in particular cubed feeds and coarse mixes) can cause problems such as colic and should be adopted over a period of time. A new foodstuff, or a different brand, may also be treated with some suspicion by a finicky feeder, which is another good reason for introducing it slowly and in small quantities.

3. Additives. Some additives have a strong smell and unless the horse is accustomed to them, he may reject the whole feed. If an unpalatable medicine or wormer has been added, this may also cause the horse to refuse all or part of his feed. Some animals actually prove to be very adept in separating what they consider to be edible from the inedible! Placing worming powders in the fridge overnight before adding them to the feed can help make the taste less offensive, whilst adding something with a strong smell or taste which the horse enjoys can help to mask the presence of extras in the feed. Treacle or honey diluted with warm water is ideal for this purpose.

4. Environment. Some horses thrive on bustle and activity in the yard, while others prefer a quieter environment, and especially so when eating. It sometimes also helps to place a greedy eater within sight of a finicky one.

5. Overfeeding. Horses on a high concentrate intake often lose their appetite at some stage. Rather than continue to present the horse with similar-sized feeds which he will probably refuse to eat, it is usually best to pursue a policy of reducing the quantity and possibly the number of feeds each day until the appetite is regained. It may also be worth consulting an equine nutritionist to decide whether alternative feeds might be used, which will supply the same energy value, but without the same bulk.

6. Container. Feeds should not be left in the stable or represented to the horse if they have been left, as they will tend to become stale and develop an unpleasant smell, especially if bran has been added. Some types of feed may even start to ferment after a period of time and could cause problems if ingested. The exception to this is if the feed is wholly comprised of cubes or coarse mix, provided they have not been moistened. Feed mangers and buckets should be scrubbed out each day to remove any traces of stale food which have become encrusted and which the horse may find offensive.

7. Quality. It should go without saying that concentrates and hay should be clean, and of good quality. Musty hay or feed past its best are unlikely to tempt a shy feeder, and in some cases may be dangerous if eaten.

8. Boredom. Although many people claim that horses are not bothered by a lack of variety in their diet, their natural grazing habits tend to belie this theory. Normally they are selective grazers, searching out the tastiest grass stems, and browsing along hedgerows for various herbs to complement the diet; and it should be remembered that grass stems are not all identical, but can vary in type as well as quality.
While it is not a good idea to change the types of foodstuff about at each feed because of upsetting the delicate balance of specialized gut bacteria, some variety can be introduced by adding various appetizers to keep the horse interested in his feed and encourage a shy feeder. These include carrots, apples, turnips, swedes, mangolds, sugar beet, cooked linseed, honey, stout, eggs and treacle. Apples, carrots, turnips, swedes and mangolds

should be sliced into fingers rather than chopped into chunks which can cause choking. Better still, they can be coarsely grated into the feed to make it more difficult for the horse to just pick out the pieces and leave the rest. Hay can be made more tempting by sprinkling it with a solution of treacle and water; this is probably easiest to do with a watering-can.

Head Banging

Head banging seems to be a rare problem, and is a response to either great physical pain or tremendous pyschological stress. The horse will lean his forehead against a stable wall and either press against it, or actually bang his head back and forth.
A vet should be asked to give the horse a thorough physical examination to discover any source of physical pain. Otherwise, the routine and general management and work the horse is being asked to perform should be looked into to decide whether this is causing sufficient stress to bring on head banging. He should be kept in as natural an environment as possible, and given the company of other horses.

Refusal to Lie Down

Horses who feel completely secure and relaxed in their surroundings will be quite happy about lying down and relaxing in the stable. Reasons why they might not do so include:

1. Too small a stable.

2. A bad experience in the past, such as being cast.

Fig 52 A horse will only lie down if he feels completely secure in his surroundings.

3. Lack of bedding.

4. Excessively soiled bedding.

5. Insecurity and lack of confidence in surroundings.

6. Some horses will not lie down while wearing rugs.

7. Illness. Horses who are seriously ill will often refuse to lie down, struggling to remain on their feet even when very weak.

8. Unfamiliarity with new surroundings.

9. Too much disturbance and activity in the yard outside the stable.

Refusal to Get Up

A horse who remains lying down when the handler enters his stable does so either because he is relaxed and confident and does not feel threatened by human presence, or because he is ill or injured. Assuming that the horse is physically well, if he continues to lie down and the handler needs to get him on his feet for some reason, the easiest method is to put a headcollar or bridle on while he is lying down. Some horses will immediately get to their feet when the handler begins to do this, in which case the problem is solved. If the horse continues to remain lying down, once the headcollar or bridle is in place, the handler can use the lead rope or reins to raise his head up and draw it a little to one side, standing well clear of the front legs as this is done. The rest of the body will generally follow the head (horses get up front end first). Do not be impatient, but give the horse time to organize his front legs underneath himself; some will pause half-way up for a stretch. Sometimes it helps to blow a raspberry, or make a buzzing noise – most horses hate the sound.

Quidding

A horse is said to be quidding when balls of partially chewed food are allowed to drop from the side of the horse's mouth while he is eating. It is normally caused by sharp teeth causing pain while chewing, or by a sore mouth, perhaps due to bit injuries, lampas or mouth ulcers. The horse will find it painful to eat food which requires much chewing, such as hay, or which is hard on the mouth, such as cubed or pelleted foods, which may be left in the bottom of the feed manger. When watching the horse eating, the handler may observe food dropping out of the mouth, and the horse will generally appear to be chewing very carefully, as though he has a mouthful of thistles.

The cause should be remedied, and in the case of a mouth injury, the horse should be either rested or ridden in a bitless bridle until the problem has cleared up. Soft, easily chewed foods should be given until

> Teeth should be checked for abnormalities and sharp edges by the vet every six months as a matter of course, and rasped if required.

the condition has been remedied, and hay can be softened by placing it in a plastic dustbin and soaking it with boiling water, the lid being replaced afterwards, and the whole being left until it has cooled before feeding it.

Refusal to Enter or Leave a Stable

A horse who refuses to enter his stable may be doing so for reasons of claustrophobia (see page 65). The box should be sufficiently large enough to give him every encouragement to enter: it often helps to turn the interior light on, especially if it is rather dark. Whitewashing the walls will also help to create a feeling of spaciousness and light.

Horses who are difficult to coax in or out of the stable may be so because of a fear of catching their heads or hips on doorways (*see* page 67) and these openings should be large enough to accommodate both horse and handler comfortably. If the horse is simply being stubborn, a sharp slap on his side (not the quarters in case he kicks out) and a firm, no-nonsense command should do the trick. When genuine fear is present, force will do little except upset the horse still further, and the chances of his injuring himself against the doorway will be increased and will thus compound his fear.

The easiest solution is either to try backing the horse in, or else use a blindfold.

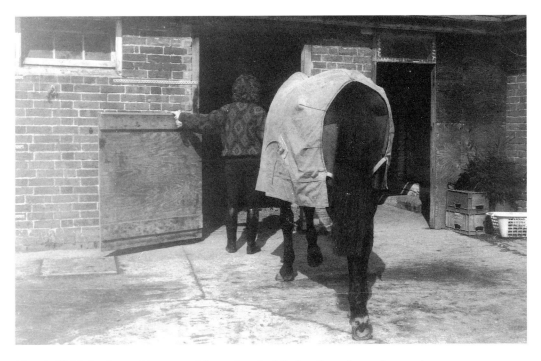

Fig 53 Hold the door wide open with one hand while leading a horse in or out of a stable in case it blows back against the horse's hips.

Care should be taken to ensure that the horse is backed into the stable in a straight line if this option is tried. A blindfold can be improvised if all else fails by using a jacket, but the handler should avoid frightening the horse while placing it over the eyes.

If the facilities are available, a stable leading directly into an enclosed yard can be used to help the horse overcome his fear: the stable door can be left open so that he can wander in and out at will, and feed times can be used as an inducement for him to move in or out of the box.

Rubbing Tail and/or Mane

A rubbed mane or tail takes time to regrow, and never looks quite so elegant afterwards. If the horse rubs his mane or tail excessively and persistently, rather than just to relieve the occasional itch, the handler should suspect some kind of irritation or discomfort in the area, and take a closer look to discover the cause:

1. In the case of rubbing the tail specifically, worms may be the problem. A regular worming programme should be observed, using an appropriate anthelmintic every six to eight weeks.

2. Lice may be present and, as with worms, it may be noticed that there is a corresponding loss of condition and the coat has a dull, dry appearance. The eggs of the lice can be seen lying in the roots of

the hair, looking very similar to small hayseeds. The affected animal and all others he is in contact with should be treated with a louse powder available either from a veterinary surgeon, or a saddler.

3. If the horse has been bathed recently, the skin (particularly if it is sensitive) may have become irritated by the shampoo used. For this reason washing-up liquid should not be used as a cheap substitute as it can be rather harsh on the skin; horses frequently seem to be less tolerant of cleansing agents used by humans. Care should be taken that all soap suds are washed out thoroughly afterwards, as if allowed to dry into the hair, it will leave the coat looking dull, scurfy and will cause itchiness.

4. Itchiness may also be caused by lazy grooming and sloppy stable management, if the skin, particularly in sensitive areas like the dock, has been allowed to remain dirty.

5. The horse may rub his tail while travelling, as well as in the stable, because he is sitting against the sides, ramp, or partitions for balance. The driver should be considerate about his four-legged passenger, and try to accelerate and brake gently, and negotiate corners at a steady speed. Protective clothing for the horse is a sensible precaution; a tail bandage and a tail guard should minimize damage to the tail hairs.

6. Sweet itch is a particularly unpleasant form of skin irritation which can cause affected animals frantically to scratch the crest, withers, and base of the tail against any available projection, sometimes until

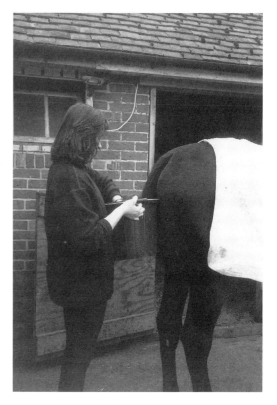

Fig 54 Care must be taken to wash all soap suds out of the tail after it has been shampooed.

it is raw and bleeding. The symptoms become apparent during the spring months and may continue through the summer until late in autumn. The condition is an allergic reaction to the bites of midges, and horses suffering from this ailment should be kept stabled during those times of the day when the midges are most active (early morning and dusk). When the horse is turned out, an effective fly repellent should be used. Severe cases may merit veterinary treatment. The mane and tail should be kept clean, and a sweet itch preparation rubbed well into the skin.

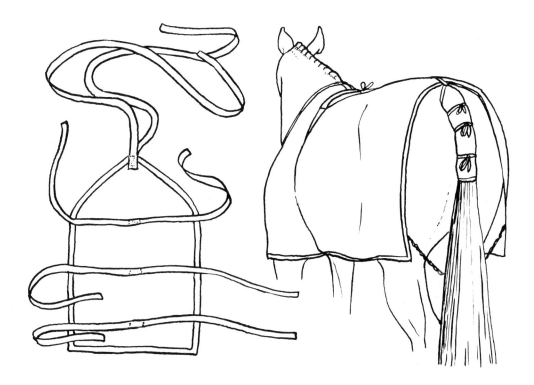

Fig 55 Tail guard.

7. Other skin problems may be at the root of the problem, and if this is suspected, seek veterinary advice.

8. The tail may be being rubbed because the horse is resting his quarters against a wall or manger, which could be a result of some kind of physical pain which he is trying to relieve. Any unusual stance should be noted, and a vet consulted and asked to examine the horse.

Rug Tearing

Rug tearing can become a very expensive habit, as well as being an inconvenient one if the horse needs to be clipped and rugged up during the winter months. It can be prevented by attaching a bib to the headcollar; this is a broad flap fitting so that it lies beneath the lower jaw, preventing the horse from catching hold of the rug with his teeth, yet allowing him to eat and drink normally.

Some horses just do not like wearing rugs, but it is worth investigating the possibility of other causes before jumping to conclusions. Youngsters may tear or chew at rugs when they are teething, for example; if you consult your vet he may be able to give you something to rub on to the gums to help ease any soreness.

Fig 56 'Bib' muzzle.

Scraping at the Ground

Some horses will paw or scrape at the ground in front of the stable door with a forefoot. In time this can begin to wear a depression on the surface of the floor, and will also wear the shoes excessively at the toe, necessitating more frequent shoeing.

It is usually caused by impatience and frustration, because the horse is waiting for his feed perhaps, or because he can see another horse leaving the yard and wishes to join him. A heavy rubber mat placed by the door will help to reduce wear on the floor and shoes, and the horse will usually desist once the source of his impatience has been removed. The habit can, however, also be caused by too much enforced idleness and confinement, so it is important to ensure that the horse receives sufficient exercise and freedom out at grass.

Weaving

Weaving is a vice most likely caused by stress, and it seems to be more highly strung and nervous horses who are most prone to developing the habit.

The horse will stand in his stable swaying from side to side, in some cases in a quite violent manner. A horse who weaves constantly is in danger of injuring his front legs; and such a horse may be unthrifty as well.

If the horse is caught weaving during the early stages, it may be possible to prevent it from developing any further, but once established, the habit will be reverted to at times of stress and anxiety. Initially, most animals will put their heads over the

Every effort should be made to ensure that rugs fit correctly and do not pinch or chafe; discomfort is often a primary cause of rug tearing. Blankets and rugs should be put on so that they lie straight, rather than uncomfortably crooked; and a late-night check will allow the handler to discover whether the horse is perhaps too hot beneath his coverings and trying to remove a few.

Bedding, especially shavings, should be brushed away from the rug lining before it is put on, as next to the skin they can be very prickly and scratchy. Some horses are also allergic to certain fibres, or to biological washing powders or fabric softners which have been used to clean the rug, and the horse may be tearing at the rug not out of a destructive tendency, but because he is attempting to scratch an irritating itch.

Fig 57 Anti-weaving grid. Note also the horse-proof bolt on the door.

door and sway from side to side, and this can be inhibited by a number of methods:

1. Fixing an upright plank to the centre of the bottom door.

2. Mounting a metal grid with a V-shaped section removed.

3. Cutting out an oval section in the top door and then closing it.

4. Suspending an old rubber tyre or half-filled plastic squash container in the centre of the doorway.

All four of these solutions allow the horse still to look over his stable door and to receive fresh air, while preventing the horse from being able to move his neck from side to side. In the case of method number 4, if he does attempt to weave, the tyre or plastic container will swing gently back against him and bump him on the side of the head. This solution does also have the merit of providing a plaything for a young horse, and some will enjoy pushing it back and forth with their noses. The drawback with all these methods, however, is that the horse may simply move back in his box and continue to weave inside, as he will do if a full grid is placed on the door; so other possibilities should be investigated as well.

Some horses may be seen to weave only at certain times, and this should be noted; feed times can commonly be a cause of stress and anxiety for the stabled horse, and so every effort should be made to ensure a regular routine in this respect. The horse should also receive exercise and liberty, and an effort made to stable youngsters where they cannot observe a confirmed weaver, lest they begin to imitate it.

The horse's personality and temperament should also be taken into consideration. Many appreciate a stable with a view across the yard, where they can see all the comings and goings; watching the everyday activity will help to prevent boredom and keep them interested. More temperamental and easily startled horses, however, may be better off in a quieter situation where there is less happening to excite or upset them. It is a case for observation and sensible assessment of the individual animal.

Fig 58 Windsucking. Some horses still succeed in doing this even with a crib strap fitted.

Fig 59 Yawning is an indication of fatigue, boredom or lack of oxygen.

Windsucking

Windsucking is a progression from crib-biting: the horse arches his neck and swallows air, except that he does not need to grasp a projecting surface with his teeth in order to do so. (*See* Crib-Biting, page 65.)

Yawning

As with humans, yawning is an indication of tiredness, boredom or lack of oxygen. The horse should receive suffi-cient exercise and/or time out in the field if boredom is suspected to be the prime cause. When stabled, the top door should be left open to ensure adequate ventilation. Where horses are kept in stables sited within a large barn, the large barn doors should be left open to encourage a flow of fresh air, provided, of course, that there is not a direct draught on to any of the occupants by doing this.

Yawning can also be caused by a blood disorder, and if it persists despite attention to the above details, a veterinary surgeon should be consulted.

CHAPTER 4

In the Field

Keeping a horse out at grass for either all, or part of the time, allows a more natural system of management, affording him the chance to socialize with others and to relax properly, both mentally and physically. Even if the horse can only be put out for a couple of hours each day, it will produce a more contented individual, better able to cope with the stresses of work.

Considering these points, it might be imagined that problems would therefore be virtually non-existent. Unfortunately, this is not the case and although there are certainly far fewer problems associated with this system of management than with the stabled horse, they can prove just as frustrating for the handler.

Biting

Although biting is also dealt with elsewhere in this book, it does sometimes occur out in the field, when the horse approaches the handler in a threatening manner. It may be caused by jealousy – perhaps another horse has just been given a titbit. No matter what the reason or cause, such behaviour must be dealt with firmly and promptly, and the horse taught that he cannot get away with such ill manners.

Alarming though the sight of a horse bearing down with his teeth bared can be, rather than backing away from the horse (which may be construed by him as submissiveness) the handler should advance towards him, shouting and waving the arms to make the horse give way, rather than the other way round. The handler should also have equipped himself with a stick, which, if the horse continues to lunge at him, can be used to give a sharp smack to the end of the horse's nose. This will usually stop the horse short in his tracks and make him think twice before trying it again.

Bullying

When a new horse is introduced to a field containing others, he may undergo a period of bullying as the herd pecking order is established. It is a sensible precaution first of all to lead the newcomer around the boundaries of the field before the other horses are then turned out with him, so that he is aware of any natural hazards and is better able to avoid getting himself into a situation where he may become cornered.

Although this can sometimes be a period of some anxiety for the owner, and a few nips may be exchanged initially, left to their own devices, the group will usually settle down in time. It is, however, sensible to leave a headcollar on the new horse in case it should become necessary to rescue him quickly; he should

Fig 60 Concentrate feeds are best given individually, even if the horse has to be removed from the field to do so, otherwise bullying is likely to occur.

of course be supervised for a while before being left.

Occasionally, an individual will be picked on mercilessly, for no apparent reason that the handler can see, and some animals may become so panic-stricken that they will even try to crash through the field fence in order to escape from their oppressor. If this seems to be the case, or serious injury is feared, it may be best to remove the horse to another field with some less aggressive company.

When hay or feeds are put out in the field, bullying frequently occurs, with the most dominant member of the group attempting to get more than his fair share. Hay should be left out in piles well separated from each other, and preferably with one pile more than the number of horses. Concentrate feeds are best given individually, even if this means having to remove each horse from the field in order to feed him to ensure that each receives his allotted ration and is not chased off by another horse.

Difficulty in Catching

This can be one of the most irritating problems a handler has to deal with, since it can involve a great deal of wasted time, and perhaps missed opportunities, too, if the horse has to be caught in time for some specific occasion such as a show.

Some horses are never any problem to catch, however hard they are worked, or badly treated. Others can pose a real problem, even if they are treated with every consideration by their owners. Although it is not a good idea to overfeed with titbits, offering a handful of nuts or similar when catching a horse (whether he is co-operative or not) does provide him with a little incentive for being caught, particularly when the grass is at its best in the early summer months.

There are several ways of dealing with horses who are difficult to catch, but the problem must be viewed not just with an immediate solution in mind, but with trying to improve the situation in future.

Fig 61 Never chase the horse, as this will only aggravate the situation and make him even more difficult.

Short Term

1. A headcollar should be left on the horse to provide something for the handler to catch hold of. It should be a close fit so as to reduce the danger of anything getting caught through it, and preferably made of supple lightweight leather which is more likely to break in such an emergency than the tougher nylon variety. Regular checks should be made to ensure that it is not chafing the head anywhere; if it does show signs of rubbing, the areas can be padded with sheepskin.

A short length of stout rope may be left attached to the central ring beneath the jawbone, which will give the handler more to hold when catching the horse, and will make it easier for him to avoid making a sudden movement towards the head.

2. Some horses will always allow greed to get the better of them in their desire not to be caught. A handful of nuts or a favourite titbit may be sufficient temptation; rustling a piece of paper in the pocket may also arouse the horse's curiosity and interest and encourage him to come close enough to discover what you have brought for him. Others are more wary, and more enticement may be needed, such as a bucket with a few nuts in the bottom, which can be rattled: most horses will

associate both the sight and the sound with feed times. Giving a few nuts to other horses in the field will sometimes provoke jealousy and greed in the recalcitrant animal, who may then decide that he does want to be caught and get his own share.

The handler should, however, take care if surrounded by a large group of horses, as sometimes a scuffle may break out amongst them as they each vie for attention and food and, obviously, the handler in the centre of it all will be in a vulnerable position.

Once the difficult horse shows interest in the food, he should be encouraged to come closer, and the handler should keep the lead rope concealed behind his back. Avoid making sudden lunges towards the headcollar as this is likely to startle the horse into backing off and adopting a wary attitude again. If carrying a bucket, hold it to the side and let the horse get his nose right in, so that the free hand can gently and quietly take hold of the side of the headcollar. Trying to grab it from the front is likely to frighten the horse; even if the handler gets a secure grip on the headcollar, he is likely to pull away and may drag the handler after him.

3. If the horse is out with others, removing them from the field first (if this is possible) will sometimes do the trick: once he realizes all his friends have gone, he may be more inclined to give in and allow himself to be caught. Never resort to chasing the horse round the field, as he is likely to interpret this as being threatening behaviour and, if still with a group of horses, will lead to the whole lot becoming excited and not in the right frame of mind for being caught.

Fig 62 Encourage the horse to approach: with some, greed overcomes the desire not to be caught.

4. With enough people to help, it may be possible to form a line across the field and gradually move forward, herding the horse into a corner. This does require quite a few people to be successful, particularly if the field is a large one. They will also need to be fairly quick on their feet if the horse is not to escape through one of the gaps in the line. There may also be a danger in that as the horse realizes that he is becoming trapped, he will either attempt to jump out of the field, or will kick out at anyone who gets too close, so he must be approached with care.

5 With fewer people available, an alternative to the above method is to take a couple of long lunge lines: each person takes hold of an end, thus forming a barrier. Again, the same hazards apply, with the additional danger that if the horse decides to try and jump the lunge line, he may become entangled with it and be brought down.

6 Hobbling or tethering are sometimes advocated for the real hardcore cases, but neither method is really ideal, and should only be used as a last resort. *(See* Appendix I, page 153).

7 When the quality and quantity of grazing improves with the warmer weather, many horses can become more difficult to catch than during the winter when there is less to keep them on the field. In the spring especially, the grass is often more tempting than any kind of special treat the handler can offer. Moving the horse to a poorer paddock will often solve the problem, but it must be ensured that the horse is receiving sufficient food.

8. Sometimes a stranger will be more successful at catching a difficult horse than the handler, since a stranger will not be associated in his mind with work, or any other experience he considers distasteful. Perhaps another person from the yard who does not normally have much contact with the horse might be persuaded to try catching him.

Long Term

The fact that a horse is difficult to catch should not be used as an excuse not to turn him out at all. Rather, the handler should try to analyse just why the horse is being awkward. If he knows that he is only caught when he is going to be ridden, he will soon become evasive, even if he is given a feed afterwards. The handler should try to visit the horse several times a day, and for no apparent reason, offering a titbit each time so that he begins to look forward to being caught rather than dreading it. If the horse is always ridden at a certain time during the day, he will also become wary about being caught at these times, and so it may be best to try and vary riding times.

Even if the horse has been difficult to catch, once he has been apprehended, the handler should praise and reward him; punishing him will only make him even more difficult in the future. It should, of course, go without saying that the handler should try to be calm and considerate when handling or working the horse, as unfair or cruel treatment will soon teach him that it is safest to stay at a distance from that person.

Escaping from the Field

Some horses are old hands at escaping from fields, especially ponies, who often

> **Safety:** Where wire fencing is used, care should be taken to ensure that the strands are kept taut, not just because sagging strands are an open invitation to escape artists, but because serious injury can result to horses or ponies if they become entangled.

seem to be particularly adept at squeezing themselves through gaps which might have been thought to be far too small. All fencing, particularly hedges, should be kept in good order, and any gaps blocked up. Even if they are too small, determined characters may push against them until they enlarge sufficiently to permit them to squeeze through. The gaps between strands of wire or rails should also be close enough together, as some horses will learn to step through them, or even to crawl underneath. Fencing should be checked each day for weak spots, which can often arise from the horse scratching himself against it, or leaning against it while trying to reach grass growing on the other side.

Some horses will escape by jumping the fence instead, and once one has learnt to do this, it can be a difficult habit to stop. Ideally the fence should be high enough to discourage the horse from attempting to jump it, but, even so, he may simply try to crash through the top of it.

The horse can be discouraged from trying either to break through fencing or to jump it by careful use of electric fence tape which can be bought by the yard

Fig 63 Gaps in hedges, such as this one, are an open invitation to escape artists.

> **Safety:** It is recommended that owners keeping horses or ponies out at grass have them freezemarked, regardless of any other precautions which may be taken to prevent or discourage theft. Freezemarking has proved to be extremely successful, and in those cases where marked animals have been stolen they are instantly and easily identifiable and usually recovered soon after. Further details about freezemarking are available from MMB Farmkey, 28 West Bar, Banbury, Oxon OX16 9RR.

(metre) and fixed to either the top or inside of the fence. This type of fencing has another advantage in that it is easily visible. Most horses have a healthy respect for electric fencing, but need to be introduced to it first by being led up to it and having their noses pressed against it so that they receive a shock. When doing this, the handler should be careful to keep his feet out of the way, as the horse may well leap backwards.

When a horse persistently escapes, it is worth giving some thought as to why he is doing so: it may be because of lack of grazing, or more commonly because he is lonely and looking for some company. As with so many problems, it is often better to treat the cause than the symptoms, and unless there is some very good reason for doing so, it is unfair to deny the horse any social intercourse.

Gate Opening

Some gate catches are easily opened by horses, which can be hazardous if he is then able to escape onto the road. Placing a padlocked chain around the gate and gatepost on the latch side will foil the most determined of horses, and will also deter horse thieves, although a similar chain and padlock should also be placed around the hinge side if the owner's main aim is to keep the horse secure from such attentions.

Refusal to Pass Through Gateways

A horse who is difficult to lead through a gateway is often so because at some time in the past, he has knocked his hips on the gatepost, or the gate has swung shut on him as he was only half-way through. All too often the handler is to blame for this situation by not opening the gate wide enough, trying instead to squeeze the horse through a narrow gap, perhaps to try and prevent other horses in the field from following through at the same time. If this is a real problem, another person should accompany the handler to help keep the other horses at bay, thereby allowing the gate to be opened wider.

The handler should also ensure that the horse has passed right through the gateway before attempting to turn him round to shut the gate, so as to avoid his catching a hip on the gatepost as he turns. Another alternative, which allows the handler to cope on his own in a situation where other horses share the grazing, is to build a catching pen in the gateway.

Sometimes the horse may be awkward because he does not like the surface: the ground in front of a gateway often becomes very poached and muddy in wet weather, with perhaps even a large puddle accumulating there (*see* page 141). The drainage in the immediate area could perhaps be improved, and some hard-stand-

Fig 64 Whether leading or riding, always ensure that gates are opened sufficiently wide enough to allow the horse to pass through without banging his hips against the gatepost. (Photo: Mike Wood)

Fig 65 Some horses may dislike the surface in a gateway, particularly if it has become very poached and soggy, or if water collects in a large puddle in the centre of it.

Fig 66 Always turn the horse's head to the gate before releasing him in case he attempts to kick out or buck.

ing put down to provide a better surface. Another reason for the horse being difficult when leaving the field may be that the horse simply does not want to leave his companions, in which case firm handling is the key (see page 125).

Kicking When Being Turned Out

Some horses will kick or buck when first turned out in the field, usually from freshness and a general joie de vivre at gaining some freedom, particularly if they do not normally get much time turned out. The fact that the horse is simply in good spirits is not a great deal of consolation to a handler who has been unfortunate (or foolhardy) enough to be on the receiving end of one of those hooves, however, and it is no more than plain common sense to take certain precautions when loosing a horse into the field.

The horse should be led into the field and the gate left slightly ajar so that the handler can easily step outside again. The horse's head should be turned towards the gate, and the handler can spend a moment or two stroking him, and perhaps offering a titbit before releasing him and stepping through the gap in the gateway.

CHAPTER 5

Under Saddle

This chapter deals primarily with difficult behaviour while being ridden, rather
than with general schooling about which
whole volumes can (and have) been writ-
ten, and on which there simply is not space
enough to deal with here. Some problems
can be extremely dangerous and, in such
cases, although suggestions are made for
attempting to remedy the situation, it is
highly recommended that the horse is
referred to an expert. If a problem is of a
nature that the confidence of the usual
rider is shaken, it is best to have a more
experienced horseman step in anyway,
since such a rider will not necessarily be
the best person to administer the correct
remedy, and may even aggravate the matter. Horses are very quick to identify a
rider's weaknesses, and will frequently
exploit them to their own ends. In many
cases, even experienced and confident riders will find it beneficial to seek tuition
from a knowledgeable instructor when
dealing with problem horses, as the underlying causes can sometimes be more
apparent to an observer on the ground
than to the mounted rider.

Riding is a hazardous activity, and it is
advisable for all riders to take suitable
safety precautions. Footwear should be
flat-soled with a raised half-inch heel; and
protective headgear, either a riding hat or
crash helmet meeting with the current
specifications laid down by the relevant

Fig 67 A good position is also a secure
and efficient one. Poor position soon
leads to evasiveness from the horse,
who learns to take advantage of the
situation, or, if the rider is actually
causing pain, attempts to resist.

Fig 68 A secure and efficient position can be acquired with the help of good, sound instruction. (Photo: Mike Wood)

authority, should be worn at all times with the chin strap correctly adjusted and fastened. Long-sleeved jackets or shirts will offer a degree of protection to the arms in the event of a fall, and when jumping or riding an unpredictable horse, a body protector is a sensible addition to the clothing. Gloves offer the rider a better purchase on the reins, especially if the latter have grips or rubber coverings. As regards the horse, all tack should be a good fit and kept well maintained and properly adjusted.

Obviously, a secure and efficient riding position acquired with the help of good, sound instruction will make it easier for a rider to overcome problem behaviour, and in some cases may prevent it from arising or becoming established. Above all, the rider should be constantly alert, since horses are quick to seize the opportunity to misbehave when they feel the rider relax his vigilance. Should the horse be startled by something rather than misbehave out of pure naughtiness, at least the rider will not be caught napping

Safety: Hard hats should be correctly fitted to each individual: the practice of borrowing a hat which does not fit properly is not one to be encouraged since it will offer as little real protection to the wearer as not wearing one at all. It should also be worn squarely on the head, not sitting on the back as is so frequently seen.

Jewellery should always be removed before riding: ear-rings (unless of the small stud type) can become caught on overhanging branches when hacking, and the lobe painfully torn; necklaces can similarly become caught up and cause serious throat injuries. Rings should be removed also, as they can not only cause blisters, but in some instances lead to the finger being ripped off.

– accidents so often happen when the rider is not concentrating on the job in hand, and open the way for bad habits to be acquired.

Bit Evasions

There are various ways in which a horse might evade the bit, including:

1. Above the bit. The horse carries his head high in the air where it is difficult for the rider to maintain control, and the action of the bit becomes ineffective. A horse who moves like this will also hollow his back, making movement inefficient and uncomfortable for both himself and his rider, and he will be unbalanced.

2. Behind the bit. The horse draws back from making a contact with the bit, the front of the face often being held behind the vertical.

3. Leaning on the bit. This frequently occurs when the horse moves with too much weight suspended over the forehand, and relies on the rider's hands for support. It is a tiring habit for the rider, and one which leads ultimately to a lack of sensitivity in the horse's mouth if allowed to persist.

4. Tongue out. Sometimes a horse may put his tongue out of the side of his mouth, either for a moment, or continuously.

5. Tongue over the bit. Instead of keeping his tongue beneath the mouthpiece of the bit, the horse draws it back and places it over the top in order to try and escape its influence.

Fig 69 Above the bit.

Fig 70 Despite the flash noseband, this horse has succeeded in putting his tongue over the bit and out of the side of his mouth. An alternative solution would be to try a grakle noseband, perhaps with the addition of a rubber tongue port attached to the bit.

6. Crossing jaws. When a contact is taken, the horse attempts to evade by crossing his jaws in a scissor-like movement.

7. Snatching. This irritating habit is when the horse frets and snatches at the bit, sometimes jerking the reins out of the rider's hands, or pulling him forward in the saddle. It may also be accompanied by jogging.

8. Opening the mouth. The horse tries to escape the action of the bit by opening his mouth; he may also lean against the contact.

When considering the best way of dealing with any bit evasion, the rider should first consider the cause behind it. If the horse is young, he may be confused and resentful of the unfamiliar feel of the bit in his mouth and will try to resist the rider's hands through lack of understanding. Attaching an extra pair of reins to the rings set on either side of a lungeing cavesson noseband will help to indicate

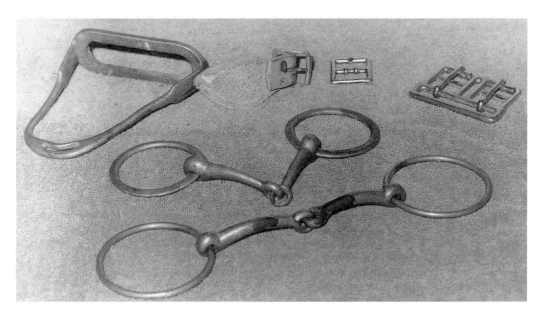

Fig 71 Worn tack is unsafe, and in the case of eroded joints and mouthpieces on bits, can cause considerable mouth problems.

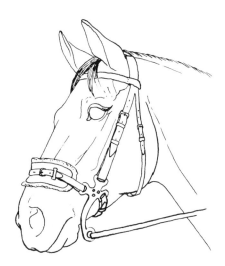

Fig 72 A few horses dislike the feel of a bit and go more happily in a bitless bridle of some description, but it must be remembered that these are potentially very severe in any but the most sensitive of hands.

the rider's wishes to the horse during initial stages of training without recourse to rough handling which will only make him more resistant. Allowing a young horse to stand idle with a bit in his mouth will also encourage him to play with the mouthpiece and perhaps discover how to draw his tongue back and place it over the top.

Rough, unsympathetic hands (sometimes as a result of the rider's lack of security and balance in the saddle) can also be a common cause of bit evasions, as can a bit which is adjusted either too high or too low in the mouth or with one side higher than the other. Worn joints or a mouthpiece which is too narrow or wide can also be a predisposing factor. Large mouthpieces can also cause discomfort in a horse who has a small mouth, while some dislike the feel of metal and work better in a rubber, vulcanite, or nylon mouthpiece.

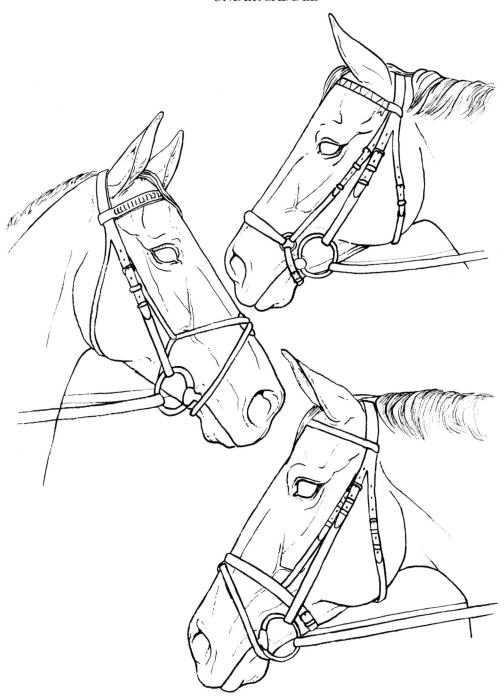

Fig 73 Clockwise from left: grakle noseband, dropped noseband, flash noseband.

Sharp teeth, teething, mouth ulcers and lampas also create discomfort in the mouth.

Once a horse has adopted a particular form of bit evasion, although the primary cause may be removed, the evasion often persists; even if the situation improves, the horse often reverts to that particular evasion at moments of stress or when he feels unco-operative or unable to meet the rider's demands, and the rider may need to use a noseband to prevent the horse from being able to evade the action of the bit when he wishes.

A dropped or flash noseband will prevent the horse from allowing his tongue to loll out of the side of his mouth, while a grakle noseband, with its higher and more concentrated pressure point on the nasal bone, is effective in preventing a horse from crossing his jaws or being able to place his tongue over the bit. In the latter case, care should be taken to ensure that the mouthpiece is not lying too low in the mouth, which may have led to the evasion in the first place. Either a dropped, flash, or grakle noseband may be used to prevent the horse from simply opening his mouth.

A horse who goes above or behind the bit, or snatches at the contact, is frequently lacking in confidence in the rider's hands, or is being over-restricted. If he leans on the bit, it is often because the rider is pushing him on too fast and onto his forehand: using half-halts and encouraging the horse to engage his quarters correctly so as to help lighten the forehand should eventually eliminate the problem with time and consistent riding. The rider should try not to pull back at the horse constantly, otherwise he will resist even more strongly.

Bolting

A horse who is bolting (as distinguished from one who gets very strong) is galloping out of control, taking little or no notice of the rider's signals. He appears to be almost in a blind panic, taking no notice of where he is going, and there have been recorded instances of such horses actually running headlong into walls and killing themselves. A confirmed bolter is not only almost impossible to cure, but is a real danger to both himself and his rider, and to passers-by and traffic. A genuine bolter does so from extreme fear and panic (the instinctive flight reaction taking precedence over all other considerations), although there are instances of brain tumours being held responsible for such behaviour, but fortunately these are relatively rare in horses.

A horse who takes a strong hold can be just as frightening and dangerous an experience for the rider, and can also be very difficult to stop. This is most likely to happen when the horse is participating in more exciting activities such as galloping, particularly in the company of others. Causes for a horse taking a strong hold and becoming out of control include:

1. Lack of schooling and obedience to the aids.

2. Over-excitement.

3. Anticipation of a gallop.

4. Overfeeding or over-fitness.

5. Incompetent or over-horsed rider.

6. Pain from badly fitting tack.

Fig 74 Cantering or galloping is an exciting activity for most horses, particularly when in company, and care should be taken not to let things get out of hand.

Prevention

As far as possible, the rider should try to avoid placing the horse in a situation where matters are likely to get out of hand, especially in the case of a horse who gets overstrong as opposed to the genuine bolter who is less predictable.

The rider should be both competent and confident of his abilities before attempting any fast work. Good going should be selected, as treacherous ground underfoot only adds to the dangers for both horse and rider. Some horses are likely to become excited and start to pull when confronted with a large, open space, but none the less this is a far safer environ-ment than cantering along grass verges where there is no room to turn if neces-sary and where there is danger from pass-ing traffic.

It is best not to ask the horse always to canter or gallop in the same place, or always when in an open space, as this will only make him anticipate such activities and make him more difficult. If it is sus-pected that the horse will get out of hand, it is best not even to attempt fast work at all until he is more obedient to the rider's wishes; and when such work is eventually tackled again, an uphill gradient will make it easier for the rider to retain con-trol. Riding with the stirrups a hole or two shorter than the usual flatwork length

---

Safety: If a horse is known to become strong, gloves should be worn to protect the palms and give a better grip on the reins, which can often become wet and slippery with sweat from the horse's neck. Gloves with pimpled rubber palms are especially good when combined with rubbered reins.

Fig 75 The rider should concentrate on maintaining an effective position if the horse does become overstrong and difficult to control.

will help the rider to keep a stronger position when he is dealing with such a problem, and if he is wearing a jacket or waistcoat, it should be zipped or buttoned up so that it does not flap around, which may frighten a nervous horse and set him off.

The rider should take care never to allow the pace he is working at to get out of hand, or encourage the horse by pushing him on faster. Racing with others only excites horses further and unnecessarily; those who become more worked up when with a group wishing to canter are best positioned at the front, rather than following on at the rear.

Emergency Action

If the worst happens and the horse does become out of control despite the rider's precautions, he should concentrate firstly on establishing and maintaining an effective position. The rider should not tip forwards: he is better able to restrain the horse by keeping the upper body upright, or slightly behind the vertical. The heels should be kept deep so that the rider is not pulled forward into a weak position; if this does happen, bridging the reins across the horse's neck will provide some support, and the horse will only be pulling against himself, rather than being able to dislodge the rider further. Unless it is absolutely imperative, the rider should not attempt to jump off: it is not easy to jump clear of a horse travelling at speed, and to do so is to invite serious injury, as well as leaving the horse entirely without any control. Neither is it ideal to head for the nearest hedge or fence, as the horse may either attempt to jump it, or crash straight through.

If there is sufficient space, the rider can attempt to steady the horse by turning him onto a large circle; as this begins to slow the pace, so the circle can be made increasingly smaller until the horse is finally back in control. It should be remembered that a large amount of space is required to execute this manoeuvre successfully, and that attempting to turn the horse on to too small a circle at too great a speed can result in his being pulled off balance and falling over.

A continuous pull on the reins is largely ineffective: the horse merely sets his jaws harder against the rider and leans on his hands for support. The rider should take sharp checks on both the reins, either at the same time, or alternately. If he finds himself being pulled forward, one hand can be anchored firmly onto the neck just above the withers, while the other hand jerks firmly on the other rein. Sometimes a sawing movement on the reins works successfully, and is likely to be more effective than a continuous pressure on the reins. If another rider has become out of control, any others who are accompanying him should follow steadily behind rather than chasing after, which will only make matters worse.

A change of bit as well as a sensible attitude to hacking and schooling is sometimes advisable. A change to a pelham or kimblewick or Dr Bristol often provides a solution if the horse is difficult to restrain in more exciting circumstances, such as competing across country. However, some horses may evade these bits by drawing their noses back in towards their chests, lessening the rider's control still more, or even by leaning downwards onto them. In these instances, a gag snaffle for a really

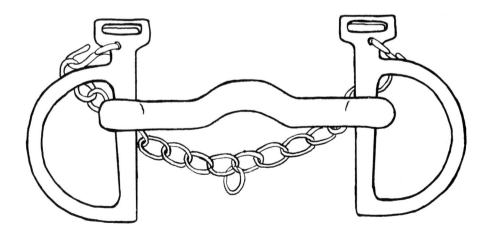

Fig 76 Kimblewick.

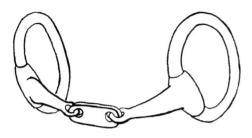

Fig 77 Dr Bristol.

determined horse may be the best answer. An alternative to a more severe bit is a Kineton, or Puckle, noseband, which exerts pressure on the front of the nose when a contact is taken on the reins.

A horse who repeatedly bolts is a danger to everyone, and is best retired from work and kept as a companion, for breeding, or else destroyed so that there is no danger

Fig 79 Puckle or Kineton noseband.

Fig 78 Pelham.

of his passing into the hands of a less competent rider.

Brushing

Brushing occurs when the horse strikes against the inside of a leg with the inside of the opposite foot while in motion. It frequently occurs because of poor conformation, but can also be caused by lack of condition, fatigue, youth, lack of fitness, or poor riding (if asked to turn in an unbalanced manner, for example).

Horses who are prone to brushing should wear brushing boots when being worked to prevent self-inflicted injuries to the inner surface of the legs. When lungeing or introducing lateral work when the chances of a knock are greatly increased, it is a sensible precaution to take anyway even if the horse does not normally brush. An eye should be kept on clenches since if they are allowed to become risen they can

> **Safety:** If brushing boots with velcro fastenings are used, they should be additionally secured by wrapping some insulating tape around them to ensure they do not work loose and move down the horse's legs.

inflict a tremendous amount of damage. If the problem is bad, it may be wise to consult the farrier, who may decide to fit feather-edged shoes which lie away from the outer edge of the hoof wall so that any damage which is inflicted is done by the hoof rather than the metal edge of the shoe.

Bucking

Although horses have been domesticated for many thousands of years now, there

Fig 80 Brushing boots.

are still occasions when they will revert to instinctive behaviour such as rearing, bolting or bucking. All of these measures were designed to preserve the equine species from being eaten by predators and they remain just as strongly developed today. Training helps to prevent such reactions from permanently keeping the upper hand, but when subjected to fear, pain or stress, instinctive behaviour frequently takes precedence.

Bucking is not a pleasant habit, although it is easy to understand: it is basically a defence mechanism, the arching of the back, lowering of the head and neck, and leap into the air, is all designed to prevent a predator from obtaining a fatal hold, and to dislodge it as quickly as possible so that the horse can then beat a hasty retreat.

Some horses will buck out of sheer high spirits and exuberance, and while it is reassuring to know that the horse is feeling well, it is not something to be encouraged in case it develops into a habit with more sinister intentions. The concentrate feed may be excessive for the horse's energy requirements, and reducing it or substituting a less heating feed may be the answer, or perhaps the horse is lacking in exercise, in which case, increasing his work and turning him out to grass for a period each day will help. A horse who is inclined to buck for these reasons may also be worked to the rider's advantage on the lunge for fifteen to twenty minutes before ridden work commences. This is often a useful policy to follow if the rider is lacking in confidence or the ability to sit a buck – the horse should not be allowed to learn that bucking can be a very effective way of removing his rider. Lungeing can also be used as a preliminary to ridden work if the horse suffers from 'cold back'

(see page 111).

If the horse has been clipped, he may well feel the cold in the winter when the stable rugs are removed before he is exercised, and this may also make him put in a buck or two. Using a woollen exercise rug and keeping the horse moving briskly will help to reduce the problem; a fillet string should, however, be attached to the back of the rug to prevent a stray gust of wind blowing it up and frightening the horse. Occasionally, a horse will buck on landing after a fence (see page 132). This is sometimes due to high spirits and excitement, but may be caused by back pain. If pain is ruled out as being the cause, the rider should not restrict the horse's headcarriage over the fence, but nevertheless must maintain a steady rein contact so that the horse does not have the opportunity to lower his head and buck on landing.

Pain caused by a physical problem, an unbalanced or awkward rider, or a pinching saddle, will also make a horse inclined to buck to try and rid himself of the discomfort, and may be evident in the general manner of going as much as by the horse trying to buck. Instead of moving freely in a relaxed way, he will generally look sour-faced, move with a stilted stride and tense hunched or hollowed back, often with the tail clamped tightly down. Some horses are also excessively ticklish, and drawing the lower leg too far back may also be a cause, especially if the horse is ridden in spurs.

Horse-fly bites during the summer are a forgivable reason for the horse putting in an unexpected buck, which is uncharacteristic, and liberal use of fly repellents is recommended to prevent such misfortunes.

Fear is sometimes a factor when placing

Fig 81 Woollen exercise rug.

a saddle on a youngster's back for the first time or girthing him up, or when he initially notices the presence of a rider on his back. Each stage of training should therefore be taken slowly with due consideration for the horse's natural fears and apprehensions if bucking is not to become an ingrained habit.

Once a horse has learnt that he can deposit the rider and thus avoid being worked, he is likely to persist in the habit until the rider takes firm steps to suppress it. Anticipation and a secure seat are all-important: a buck can usually be nipped in the bud if the rider is prepared for the warning signals – the head beginning to lower and the back muscles starting to lift and bunch up. In order to buck effectively, the horse must slow down, lower his head and transfer his weight to the forehand. To prevent this from happening, the rider should bring his

Fig 82 Bridging the reins.

upper body upright or slightly behind the vertical, taking a firm contact on both reins and raising the horse's head as much as possible. The lower leg should be kept braced slightly forward with the heel deep so that the rider is not thrown forward into a vulnerable and insecure position. Bridging the reins if the rider is inadvertently thrown forward will help as they will form a support against the horse's neck, which the rider can use to help regain his balance. A slightly shorter stirrup than usual will also help, and the rider should try to keep the horse active and his quarters engaged since it is more difficult for a horse to buck if he is travelling forwards briskly. Working the horse

on a circle also helps as he will have to concentrate more on keeping his balance; the circle also has the additional benefit of creating more activity behind.

Small ponies can sometimes present a problem, as young children do not always have the security of seat (or presence of mind) to cope adequately. The lack of strength may also cause difficulty as they may not physically be able to raise the head when the pony tries to lower it. Fitting grass reins will be of assistance in this case: they consist of a piece of cord clipped to the bit rings, passing through the loops at the end of the browband, and back to the D-rings on the front of the saddle. These can also be of great help if the pony tends to try and roll during exercise (see page 126).

Hitting the horse with a whip is not generally recommended as a remedy, as if anything it is more likely to cause the horse to buck more in self-defence, particularly if it is used behind the saddle.

Catching Hold of Reins, Bit Cheekpieces, or Martingale

This habit often starts when the horse is young and teething, when he is inclined to grab hold of something. It can be poten-tially dangerous, as the horse may get a tooth caught up and frighten or unbalance himself, as well as removing the rider's control over the situation.

When mounting, the rider should try to keep a contact (not a backwards pull) on the reins to prevent the horse from being able to turn his head and snatch at the rein. If a bit with cheekpieces is necessary, these can be coated with an unpleasant-tasting substance such as bitter aloes; the same remedy can be used on the reins as well if necessary.

If the horse grabs at the straps of a running martingale, a bib martingale can be

Fig 83 Catching hold of the reins with the teeth is a habit which often starts when the horse is young, but can be potentially dangerous if a tooth becomes caught up.

Fig 84 An incorrect canter lead, especially when riding a turn or circle, as seen here, results in loss of balance.

used instead. The design is basically the same, except that a flap of leather is stitched between the two straps which run to the reins. Although it will not prevent the horse from being able to grab hold of it, it does eliminate the danger of a tooth becoming caught.

Changing Canter Leads

Some horses will change canter leads when working in this gait. The horse may change completely, or else only partially, leading to an incorrect sequence of movement of the legs. This latter fault is termed disunited, where the horse has changed either in front or behind. The cor-rect sequence of movement should be near hind, off hind and near fore together, then off fore (when cantering on the right rein); and off hind, near hind and off fore together, then near fore (when cantering on the left rein). A change in this se-quence of movement produces a bumpy motion, and the horse will be very unba-lanced, particularly when executing a turn or circle. Even if the horse changes his canter leads all round, he will still be unbalanced and inclined to prop onto his inside shoulder around turns and circles.

The problem commonly occurs in young horses who are unaccustomed to carrying a rider's weight, and it generally resolves itself with increased maturity and

Safety: The rider should not persist in cantering if the horse is on the wrong lead, or becomes disunited, but rather return to trot and then re-establish correct canter other-wise there is a very real danger that the horse may lose his footing and fall, especially if executing a turn, circle, or on slippery going.

Fig 85 Sequence of movement for canter with left foreleg leading: off hind, near hind and off fore together, near fore, followed by a moment of suspension before the sequence begins again. The correct sequence for canter with the right foreleg leading is: near hind, off hind and near fore together, off fore, followed by a moment of suspension.

strength, but it can also be caused by an unbalanced rider, asking for too great a degree of collection before the horse is ready, unco-ordinated or rough hand movements, or attempting to ride too small a circle or too deep a corner for the horse's level of ability. Horses who are being taught counter-canter or flying changes may also develop this habit, particularly if the rider suddenly changes his weight distribution or sits crookedly.

Some horses may be particularly stiff to one rein, and will find it difficult to canter on the correct lead in one particular direction, and having achieved it, will attempt to change back to the more comfortable lead. If the horse is suffering from a physical problem which makes it painful to canter on the desired lead, an examination by a veterinary surgeon should determine the root of the problem.

If the horse changes his canter lead either entirely or partially, without being requested to, the rider should quietly return him to trot and ask him to strike off again in a calm and balanced manner. Using a circle to help position the horse and encourage a small amount of inside bend often helps, or popping him over a small fence positioned in a corner of the school will generally encourage the horse to strike off correctly.

Clumsiness and Stumbling

Although some horses are naturally more athletic and agile than others, clumsiness is most often due to weakness and lack of muscular strength, either because of youth, or perhaps because the horse has been out of work for some time. Clumsiness can also be the result of a lack of schooling, poor shoeing, debility, and tiredness. If these conditions are eliminated, there is a possibility that it is caused by some kind of physical problem such as a back injury or nervous disorder.

Stumbling may have similar causes, or be because a stone has become lodged in a

Fig 86 Horses disposed to moving on the forehand (top) are more likely to
stumble than if ridden positively forward with impulsion and a correct
rhythm. The rider should also check that he is not tipping forward and
overloading the forehand even more.

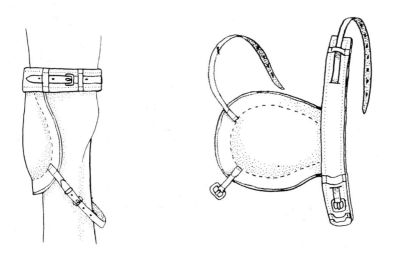

Fig 87 Knee boots.

foot, or perhaps because the horse has thin or flat soles and is being worked on stony ground. It is sometimes the result of a lack of concentration, the horse not paying sufficient attention to where he is going. The rider should ensure the horse is moving actively, and into a positive contact, since if he tends to work on his forehand, this will predispose him to stumbling. Shoeing with rolled toes may help, and the horse should be ridden in knee boots in case he does come down and injures the joints.

Cold Back

Various theories have been put forward to explain the condition described as 'cold back' including poorly fitting tack, previous rib/sternum fractures, the pressure of the girth being tightened causing a sudden drop of blood pressure, and panic reactions. Whatever the cause, the symptoms vary from the horse hunching and tensing his back as the girth is tightened and tension being apparent in his movements for a period thereafter, to a sinking of the back, with it sometimes sagging until the belly nearly touches the ground, or collapsing unexpectedly. Some may then become explosive, bucking and plunging.

Using a thick, fleecy numnah beneath the saddle seems to help slightly, and the girth should be left just firmly fastened

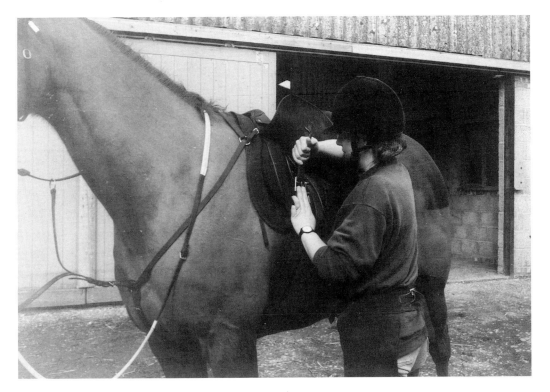

Fig 88 The girth should be tightened gently and gradually.

enough to keep the saddle in place initially. It should be tightened gently, rather than abruptly. The saddle can be left loosely girthed up for about ten minutes before preparing to ride the horse, when the girth can gradually and carefully be tightened again. Often, walking the horse around in hand for five minutes or so before finally tightening the girth and mounting seems to help.

Difficulty in Mounting/ Dismounting

Mounting

Horses who are fidgety, refusing to stand still to be mounted, or who attempt to nip while the rider is getting on may be so because they are badly trained, but more frequently become difficult because of sloppy, or awkward mounting by the rider. This in turn leads to sore backs and progressively less co-operative behaviour from the horse.

Assuming that the rider is athletic and correct in his mounting technique, and that the horse has simply not been trained properly to stand still while being mounted, a great deal of patience will be required. The rider should make as though to mount, and if the horse starts to move or fidget, cease and insist that he stands still again before recommencing. Each time the horse moves, the rider should give him the command 'Stand', praising him when he does so. An assistant can often be helpful in encouraging

Fig 89 The rider should try to be as athletic as possible, using the mane for support rather than the front of the saddle, and reaching for the far side of the waist of the saddle as he springs upwards.

the horse to stand still while being mounted during the early stages, but if one is unavailable, positioning him so that he is close to a wall or fence may help. If the horse tends to move backwards, he should be positioned with his quarters facing towards the barrier; if he steps to the side, he should be positioned so that he is alongside the wall, and so on.

Poor mounting is the most common cause for a fidgety horse, or one who nips, so the rider should be careful not to stick a toe in his ribs, or to land heavily in the saddle. Holding the reins too tightly or pulling back on them for balance will almost certainly encourage the horse to move backwards, while if the rider kicks the horse on the quarters while swinging the right leg over his back, or drags the saddle to one side, the horse cannot be blamed for becoming awkward. A girth which is pinching the sensitive skin behind the elbows because the forelegs have not been stretched forwards can also be responsible for discomfort, as can a badly fitting saddle.

The rider should try to be athletic when mounting, so as to cause as little discomfort as possible. A handful of mane should be held in the left hand together with the reins, and used for support rather than the front of the saddle or the horse's mouth. As the rider springs up, he should reach for the far side of the waist of the

Fig 90 A mounting block is useful for shorter or less athletic riders: this particular model is available in two sizes weighing 35lb (15.8kg) or 48lb (21.7kg) from Martello Plastics, 57–59 Canterbury Road, Folkestone, Kent. (Photo: Courtesy of Martello Plastics)

saddle, rather than the cantle: this will reduce the danger of the saddle slipping to one side, injury to the back muscles, or damage to the internal structure of the saddle itself. Insisting that the horse stands squarely will also ensure that he is standing in a balanced manner and will be less likely to move when the rider attempts to mount.

If the horse is very large and the rider very short, or if the rider is very stiff for some reason, it is often best for both if a mounting block is used. In the case of a horse who tries to nip when the rider mounts, the offside rein can be held very slightly shorter than the nearside one, so that the horse is unable to reach the rider with his teeth. However, the rein should not be held so tightly that the horse is unbalanced. The cause of the problem, most often poor mounting, should also be remedied, rather than just prevented.

Back pain can also be responsible for the horse becoming difficult, and if this is suspected, a veterinary surgeon should be requested to examine the animal.

Dismounting

Difficulties in dismounting are less frequent than in mounting, although they often have the same causes: discomfort caused by tack or rider, or fear – perhaps the horse has been badly frightened in the past while being dismounted, which it continues to identify with this activity.

The rider should be as careful about dismounting correctly as mounting. The safest method, which gives least discomfort to the horse, is to remove both feet from the stirrups and, taking the reins in the left hand, place the right hand on the pommel of the saddle for support while the

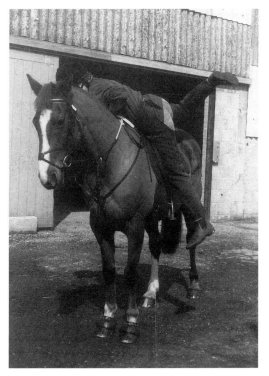

Fig 91 When dismounting, the rider should remove both feet from the stirrup irons and vault lightly off, making sure that the right leg does not become caught around the back of the saddle or catch the horse's quarters.

rider vaults off. Pulling backwards on the reins or jerking them when dismounting, or failing to clear the back of the saddle or quarters with the right foot will all cause a horse discomfort and make him shift restlessly. Dismounting cowboy-style, leaving the left foot in the stirrup can result in a toe sticking into the horse's side, and also pulls the saddle across to one side, not only causing pain, but unbalancing the horse, who then has to move in order to brace himself better. More seriously still, should the horse take exception to being dismounted, or if he is startled, the rider's

Fig 92 Dismounting cowboy-style can be extremely dangerous if the horse is startled and moves suddenly.

left foot can become trapped in the stirrup, and should the horse then panic and actually try to run off, the rider may be dragged behind him and either trampled or kicked.

The rider will also need a great deal of patience when dealing with a horse who is apprehensive or difficult about being dismounted. If the horse starts to move when the rider is attempting to dismount, he should resume his position and quietly insist that he stands still before starting to dismount again. An assistant to hold the horse (by the noseband rather than the bit) can also be a big help.

It is worth checking the fit of the saddle, since if it is low on the withers or too narrow and pinching, it will cause great discomfort when the rider supports his weight on the pommel.

Forging

Forging occurs when the toe of a hind shoe catches the underside of a foreshoe on the same side, making a distinctive clicking noise. It is most common at trot in young, unbalanced, unfit, or tired horses, or when the rider allows the horse to run along on his forehand. With schooling, improved balance and muscular strength, fitness and co-ordination, the habit usually disappears. The rider should beware of pushing the horse on too fast, and should use half-halts to achieve a better balance and rhythm.

It may persist to a degree in horses with very short backs, in which case shoeing behind with rolled toes may help.

Headshaking

Headshaking can be an irritating habit for the rider, in severe cases leading to a

Fig 93 Forging: the toe of a hind shoe strikes the shoe of the hoof in front.

painful bang on the nose and the reins being jerked out of his hands. The horse's behaviour can vary from a slight twitch of the head from side to side, or slight nod, to pronounced and vigorous up and down movements; he may try to rub his nose against his forelimbs, or even try and strike out with the forelegs.

If it appears to be an intentional movement, it may be that the problem is caused by a badly fitting bridle: a browband which is too short and pulls the headpiece forwards into the base of the ears, a noseband (particularly grakle or dropped nosebands) in which the cheekpiece lies uncomfortably close to the eyes, or a worn or ill-fitting bit. It may also be caused by a heavy-handed rider. In the summer, flies can be responsible for a great deal of irritation, although a fly fringe combined with the use of an effective repellant usually solves the problem.

If the movement appears to be an uncontrolled, involuntary one, it may be caused by some kind of physical problem, such as earache or toothache, parasites or hayseeds in the ears, sinus and throat problems. If the habit persists, a vet should be asked to examine the horse.

There are cases where there are no obvious clinical reasons for headshaking, and these can prove extremely frustrating since it is difficult to determine a suitable remedy. Many horses who have started headshaking have been reported as showing worse symptoms during warm or bright weather, and improving when it is overcast, cool, or when working in the confines of an indoor school. Explanations put forward for this include possible allergic reactions, or a hypersensitivity to ultraviolet light. Some people have achieved a measure of success in these cir-

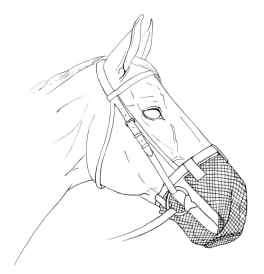

Fig 94 Some people have achieved a degree of success with headshakers by attaching a muslin net to the bridle noseband, which covers the horse's muzzle.

cumstances by attaching a muslin net to the noseband, which covers the muzzle, allowing the horse to breathe freely, but which acts as a primitive filter. It is not known why this should apparently help some horses, as the habit is still, as yet, poorly understood.

Jogging

Horses who persistently jog can be tiring and uncomfortable for the rider. The habit is most common in those horses who are overfed and under-exercised, or those who are of an excitable nature. The problem can also arise as a result of the rider pushing the horse on too fast in walk, or through insensitive riding, usually when too much hand and leg are applied simultaneously. Giving the horse more exercise,

Fig 95 Horses who persistently jog can be tiring and uncomfortable for the
rider, but it can be caused by a poor rider position in the first place,
particularly if the lower leg grips upwards on a sensitive horse.

preferably combined with time out at grass each day and adopting a lower-energy diet may be the solution to the first cause. Riding out in the company of a more placid horse may also prove to have a calming effect on an excitable horse and, when riding in company, he is usually more settled when taking the lead or moving alongside the lead horse. If the problem is caused by insensitive riding, steps should be taken to remedy this, preferably with the help of an experienced instructor. The rider will need to exercise tact, soothing the horse with his voice when he breaks into a jog, and gently applying half-halts. Care should be taken not to make the horse feel over-restricted by the contact and schooling aimed at encouraging the horse to accept the pressure of the rider's legs rather than running from them.

The position of the rider may also need some attention: if this is sloppy or very tense, perhaps with a gripping lower leg, the horse may try to escape from the discomfort by jogging. Discomfort caused by a poorly fitting saddle may also make the horse jog.

Laziness

There may be very good reasons for a

horse exhibiting signs of laziness: he may be tired (especially if he is not particularly fit to start with, he will tire quickly); he may be physically immature or weak, thus finding it hard to work correctly while supporting the weight of a rider; he may be being asked to carry a rider who is too heavy for him; or he may be old or underfed for the amount of work he is asked to do. A physical reason may be to blame also and, if this is suspected, a vet should be consulted and blood samples taken to try to determine the cause of the lethargy.

Some horses do not enjoy particular types of work such as jumping or flatwork, and while displaying idleness when working in a school or *manège*, will brighten up when given the stimulus of different surroundings or taken out hacking. In such cases, schooling should be made as varied and interesting as possible, preferably in the company of other horses, and such sessions kept brief. A great deal of schooling can be done while out hacking and, particularly if the horse displays a marked lack of enthusiasm for school work, this is often a good policy to follow.

Mareishness

Some mares can be unpredictable in their performance and behaviour, most noticeably so when in season, which is presumably due to the variation of concentrations of hormones at different stages of the oestrous cycle. They may be reluctant to move forward, will repeatedly pass small quantities of urine, will 'wink' the clitoris, may refuse to jump, and may become uncharacteristically irritable and difficult to handle generally, swishing the tail and perhaps with a tendency to kick. In

extreme cases, the problem can be resolved by administering a drug which suppresses the oestrous cycle; a veterinary surgeon should be consulted if the rider feels that this course of action is appropriate.

Nappiness

Napping is an age-old problem, which can arise from a variety of causes, most commonly:

1. The horse may be challenging the authority of the handler.

2. He may be reluctant to leave a group of other horses, or his yard (see page 125.)

3. He may be confused by, or unable to meet, the demands of the rider, or he may be being given imprecise aids.

4. Weakness, fatigue, overwork, or feeling off-colour.

5. The horse may be lazy and ungenerous in his temperament, unwilling to co-operate with the rider's wishes.

A nappy horse will remain rooted to the spot, his forelegs braced, ignoring the rider's aids to move forward. If the rider becomes insistent, he may show signs of temper, his ears being laid back and the tail swishing violently, and he may kick out, buck on the spot, try to run backwards, swing around back in the direction he has come from, or rear. Few horses are born nappy, but become that way because of the manner in which they are handled, although a few genuine rogues do exist

Fig 96 Nappiness (top) often needs firm handling and riding forward (bottom).

and the herd instinct seems to be more strongly developed in some individuals than others, leading to a reluctance to leave their companions. What may initially start out as genuine worry and anxiety can rapidly develop into a challenge to the rider's authority at every given opportunity unless the causes are identified and the horse sensitively but firmly dealt with at the first signs.

Horses have excellent memories and, allowed to get away with an evasion just once, it is highly likely that it will be tried out again at some point in the future: it may be found that a horse will particularly associate a certain place with napping, and will do so repeatedly each time he is there. Fear can also be responsible for a horse napping; an unusual scent or object can stop him in his tracks and he will be reluctant to pass. A certain amount of tolerance and understanding must be applied by the rider in such circumstances: while the horse must be encouraged to move past the source of his fear, the rider should not compound his anxieties through rough, bullying tactics, but rather attempt to allay his fears by being soothing as well as firm, giving the horse time to come to terms with his worries. The more confidence the horse has in his rider, the less of a problem this will be.

Nappiness frequently starts in youth as part of the growing-up process: as they begin to feel their strength, they may test out their rider to see just how much they can get away with. The rider should also be careful to introduce new experiences and exercises gradually so that the horse can develop confidence and becomes used to accepting the authority of the rider: he should not be placed in a situation where he is likely to rebel. Demanding too much too soon quickly leads to mutiny if the horse feels psychologically overstretched, insecure, or tired. Pain caused by a physical infirmity, ill-fitting tack, or poor riding will also cause the horse to look for ways of avoiding work.

A nervous or inexperienced rider can contribute to the problem. Most horses are quick to discover that they can not only get away with such unacceptable behaviour, but will receive little correction for it. Napping can also be attributed to a direct fault of the rider, always taking the same route when hacking, for example, or simply going a certain distance and doubling back on his tracks, or even spending a set length of time on schooling. The horse anticipates turning for home at a certain point, or the finish of school work, and becomes resentful when the rider wishes to continue.

There is no one perfect cure for nappiness once the trait has become established, and although the habit can be corrected to a certain extent, the tendency will still remain and is likely to resurface on those occasions when the horse feels stressed or pressurized, or when a new rider gets on his back.

The rider should attempt to keep the horse active and moving forward when he tries to nap, and particularly should try to keep him from running backwards, which cannot only be dangerous, but lead to rearing. At the first evidence of hesitation, the rider should apply legs, seat, voice (a firm command rather than shrieking) and, if necessary, stick. If it is likely to be difficult to free one hand from the reins in order to use the stick, a long schooling whip should be carried instead, or perhaps spurs worn. When schooling, the rider should aim at making the horse as obedient and responsive to the leg aids as possible, to make it easier to overcome this type of resistance. If the horse's reaction is to kick out or buck, it may be best to return to basics anyway, teaching him to accept and obey the leg aids rather than resist them. If the horse tries to buck (see page 103), the rider should try to keep his head up, as this will limit his ability to do so.

The rider should try to keep the horse straight and prevent him from evading by swinging around on his quarters. Provided he can be kept straight, if he resists the leg aids in one of the above-mentioned ways, it is sometimes best not to be over-insistent with them: often, just keeping the horse standing still, facing the direction the rider wishes to go in until he shows signs of restlessness and wanting to move on again works quite successfully, although sitting it out in this manner may take some time, and progress initially may be rather halting. Eventually though, the horse will become bored and will soon come to realize that it is preferable to continue.

If the horse attempts to swing around, rear, walk backwards, or if time is short and it is necessary to try and induce some kind of movement, a different tactic can be tried. Circling the horse tightly will shift him in a sideways direction, from which the rider can try to re-establish forwards movement. Circling the horse several times, while using plenty of leg to keep him active and up to the bridle will prevent him from running backwards, and while he is on the move, he will be unable to rear.

If the horse attempts to swing around to the right, and the rider is unable to prevent him in time, it is usually easiest to follow the line of least resistance, and to circle him in this manner to the right, and vice versa. After a few circles (care should be taken on slippery surfaces when executing this manoeuvre) the horse can be straightened to the original direction once more and the horse asked to move forwards again. If he resists once more, he should be circled again, and the exercise repeated as many times as necessary. Once the horse does move forward, he should be pushed on briskly, keeping him between hand and leg. Having established forward movement, the horse can then be praised with a pat and a few words.

It is important to leave plenty of time if it is anticipated that the horse will be

---

Safety: Napping can be potentially hazardous if it happens on a busy road, particularly if the horse is inclined to try and run backwards, kick out, or buck. For these reasons, the rider should never attempt to correct a horse on such roads. It is often helpful to have an assistant follow on foot or on a bicycle, if napping only occurs while out hacking, who will be able to control traffic if necessary, as well as encourage the horse forward. If an assistant is unavailable, long-reining along quiet lanes can sometimes help to overcome this problem, since the rider is in a better position to drive the horse forward when he naps.

Fig 97 Sometimes teaching the horse to long-rein can be a means of overcoming nappiness.

nappy: giving in and turning for home is an open admission of defeat by the rider, and the horse will be even more difficult the next time. The rider should also try not to get in front of the movement, but adopt an upright and positive position be able to ride the horse forward most effectively (*see* also page 123 and page 125).

Over-Excitement

Horses may become over-excited in certain situations, such as in the bustle of a show atmosphere, or when hunting. It may be caused by the tension present in the atmosphere, perhaps aggravated by the rider's own excitement and tension, or perhaps caused by anticipation of an exciting activity such as jumping at speed. If the horse is lacking in social intercourse with his own kind, the mere presence of other horses may be enough to excite him, particularly if he has a nervous or highly strung temperament.

Working the horse and turning him out regularly in the company of others will help to dispel much of the excitement which occurs when he is with groups of other horses and riders. Initially, it may be best with youngsters, to introduce them to shows by competing in the early classes first thing in the morning, when the show ground is generally much quieter and there is less to upset the horses. Finding a quiet corner to work in is often preferable to braving the hurly burly of a busy collecting ring, and it will be easier to settle and relax the horse. Frequently, it is found that the more the horse is exposed to such environments, the more quickly he will relax and concentrate on his job, provided, of course, that he is sensibly ridden.

Over-Reaching

This is caused by the toe of a rear shoe striking down into the heel of a forefoot. Over-reaching most commonly occurs when the horse is doing fast work or jumping, particularly if he is asked to stop abruptly, turn tightly or move across uneven or deep going. Horses with poor conformation such as short backs or sickle hocks are more susceptible, but overlong toes, lack of schooling and fatigue can also be to blame.

Correct riding, maintaining the horse in balance between hand and leg and with a regard for the going will help prevent over-reaching in many circumstances, but as an added precaution the horse can be shod behind with rolled toes, and over-

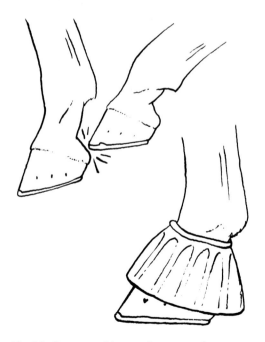

Fig 98 Over-reaching and over-reach boots.

Fig 99 Care should be taken when riding on uneven going or downward inclines, as there is an increased danger of over-reaching.

reach boots fitted in front. If the horse is unused to wearing over-reach boots and has a sensitive skin, a little petroleum-jelly smeared around the top inside edge will allow them to slide, rather than chafe.

Rearing

Rearing is perhaps one of the most dangerous and unpleasant vices which a horse may have and it can be difficult to try and effect a remedy. Dealing with such horses should very much be left to the expert; it is not a problem which a novice, inexperienced, or less than confident rider should try and handle himself.

When the horse does rear, there is a very real danger that if he goes up very high, he may lose his balance and topple over backwards, possibly trapping the rider

Safety: Care should be taken not to use over-reach boots that are too large for the horse or pony. If they are too long the toe of a back foot may step onto the heel of a boot and trip the horse up. If necessary, any excess length can be trimmed off using a pair of scissors.

Fig 100 Rearing may sometimes be caused by asking for too great a degree of collection which the horse cannot comfortably cope with, especially if the rider restricts too much with the hands.

underneath as well as inviting damage to the horse's saddle and back. The rider should therefore make every possible effort to stay forward with the horse and he must be especially careful not to pull backwards on the horse's mouth, which will pull him off balance. Placing the arms around the horse's neck will help the rider to maintain a forward position without interfering with the horse's balance, and as soon as his front feet touch the ground again, he should be strongly urged forward.

If the horse begins to lose his balance and if the rider has sufficient presence of mind, he should slip both feet free of the stirrups and slide off to one side rather than risk the horse falling on him, but this does require quick thinking and even quicker reactions.

Sometimes the threat to rear can be forestalled by the rider. In order to rear, the horse must first stop and lift his head, so when the rider feels the horse slowing, the quarters lowering and the front feet beginning to lift from the ground, he should circle the horse tightly so as to maintain forward impulsion with the rider's inside hand maintaining a definite inside bend through the neck, and carried low to prevent the horse from being able to raise his head.

Some horses will rear because of nappiness, stubbornness or laziness, also because of too severe a bit in a sensitive mouth, a rough-handed rider, or because he is being asked for a greater degree of collection than he can comfortably cope with. Some horses seem particularly to resent hackamore bridles, and many riders seem unaware of their potential severity, assuming that they must be milder because there is no mouthpiece. A solution is sometimes to develop a more sympathetic hand and to use a milder bit. Avoiding asking for more collected work which encourages the horse to transfer his weight to his quarters may also help avert trouble *(see* pages 117–18).

Refusal to Leave Home or Other Horses

Refusing to leave home, or other horses, can be an exasperating problem, usually stemming from a lack of security and confidence in the rider (the horse feels safest in his own familiar environment, or amongst companions).

Teaching the horse to leave his friends should start when he is still young: once the foal has been taught to lead while following his dam, he can then be led at gradually increasing distances away from her, so that he learns to follow the handler, rather than his mother's tail.

An adult horse can pose more of a problem, being considerably larger and stronger. If he normally works in an environment such as a riding school where much of the work tends to be of a follow-my-leader fashion, an effort should be made to incorporate exercises such as passing the rest of the ride on the inside, working on the opposite rein against the ride and so forth, so that following other horses does not become an ingrained habit. This will also teach him to be more

Fig 101 The 'herd instinct' can be utilized when dealing with a horse who is reluctant to leave home. A school master can be used to encourage the horse to follow after initially and, gradually, he can be asked to work alongside and eventually in the lead.

receptive to the rider's aids, as well as teaching the rider a little more control.

The horse may need firm, very positive riding, the leg aids reinforced if needs be by a whip, but he should not be beaten into submission. The horse must learn to obey the rider's wishes, but must also develop confidence in him, which will not be achieved by brute force alone. When the rider is faced with hacking the horse out of the yard, it helps initially to have the assistance of a sensible and well-

Fig 102 After a period of retraining, the two horses can go out and at some
point on the route, take diverging roads to return home separately.

mannered horse. He can then be encouraged to leave the yard following his companion, and gradually encouraged to work alongside him. The horse can then be progressively made to take the lead, rather than follow all the time. Ultimately, after a period of retraining, the two horses can go out and at some point on the route, take diverging roads, to return home separately. It helps if the first time this is attempted, the problem horse is turned onto a road which leads back towards home, so that the temptation to nap back towards his companion is lessened. If another horse is not available, it may be beneficial to teach the horse to long-rein, so that the rider is in a position to drive him forward when he attempts to nap back towards the yard (*see* page 118).

Rolling

Rolling is a normal action for a horse, allowing him to acquire an insulating coat of mud when he is cold, helping him to cool down when he is hot or sweaty, and an enjoyable way of relieving an itch. However, some horses will attempt to roll while being ridden, which can be dangerous for the rider, who may be trapped underneath, as well as damaging the saddle, and possibly the horse's back as he rolls over the hard structures within the saddle.

Horses are most likely to attempt to roll when they are hot and sweaty, when going through, or standing in, water, or when finding themselves on a particularly inviting looking patch of soft sand or possibly the surface of an indoor or outdoor riding surface. Some horses will also persist in this habit if they have been successful in the past, realizing that they can easily rid themselves of the rider.

The first sign that the horse is about to roll is a lowering of his head and pawing at the ground, followed by buckling at the knees. When a horse lies down, he does so front end first, so if the rider can keep his head up and ride him strongly forward, the danger can be averted. Legs, voice and whip, if necessary, can all be used to urge the horse forward and keep him moving. Small children may not be strong enough to keep a pony's head up, in which case grass reins (a piece of cord attached to the bit rings, running through the loop at the end of the browband and back to the front D-rings on the saddle) will help to prevent the pony from being able to lower his head enough to lie down.

Should the rider not be quick, or alert, enough to prevent the horse from going down, he should kick both feet free of the stirrups and jump off quickly to the side to avoid becoming trapped beneath the horse. If it is safe to do so, the rider should try to keep hold of the reins to prevent the horse from getting his front legs entangled in them, and as soon as possible he should use them to raise the horse's head and get him to his feet before he can roll on the saddle.

Rubbing the Rider Off

An unpleasant and dangerous habit is that of the horse trying to rid himself of the rider by trying to rub him off against a fence, wall, or tree. The rider should try to avoid allowing the horse to get too close to fences, walls, etc., and when riding in a

Fig 103 Schooling the horse on an inner track away from the fence.

school or *manège* should work the horse at a short distance away from the outer track. The whip should be carried in the outside hand, rather than the inside one as is normally recommended so that it can be used to discourage the horse from making a dive towards the wall or kicking boards. The moment the horse does try to move towards a barrier, the rider should use the leg on that side strongly, backed up if necessary by the whip on his shoulder.

Schooling should be aimed at trying to make the horse as obedient as possible to the leg aids but, even so, the rider will need to remain alert: if the horse is really determined, spurs may be necessary, although they should only be used when the horse attempts to dislodge the rider in this way.

Shying

Shying is a natural reaction to a frightening or unfamiliar object: the horse will be reluctant to approach it, and when made to go past will try to keep plenty of distance between himself and the object, keeping a wary eye on it and possibly trying to rush past as quickly as possible as he draws level. It can also be due to overfreshness, in which case a lower-energy concentrate feed should perhaps be considered, plus more exercise and time allowed out at grass. Another cause can be poor vision, and if the problem is a frequent one, a vet should be asked to examine the eyesight.

It is a habit which is potentially dangerous when riding on roads, since the horse may shy away from an object on the verge or kerb, and into the path of passing traffic. While riding, and especially so when on the roads, the rider should therefore remain alert at all times, keeping the horse between hand and leg. Once a horse has shied at a particular place, he may well shy at that same point every time thereafter, anticipating the frightening object still being there. The rider should remain calm and firm, and not tense up when approaching such spots, or when feeling the horse beginning to spook, as he will only agitate him further. A soothing voice may help to reassure a genuinely anxious horse, combined with positive – not aggressive – riding.

As the horse begins to shy, his pace will begin to slow, the steps becoming shorter, more hesitant, and sometimes more elevated, and the body swinging away from the object which worries him. If the rider is not quick to anticipate, the horse may try to swing around and move off in the opposite direction.

Fig 104 Especially on the roads, the rider should remain alert at all times in case the horse shies at an unfamiliar or frightening object.

If traffic is approaching from either direction, the rider should not attempt to make the horse move forward past the object until the road is clear, in case the horse swings his quarters into the centre of the road. Sometimes, having halted and allowed the horse to take a good look at the object of his fear, he will be reassured and will walk past warily, but obediently.

Provided the road is clear, the rider can ask the horse to walk calmly forwards. Rather than pulling on the left rein to try and keep the horse close to the kerb, which will result in his swinging his

Fig 105 If the horse shies at an object by the side of the road, the rider should use the right rein and right leg to bend the horse towards the object in order to prevent the quarters from swinging out into the path of passing vehicles.

quarters out into the road, the rider should use the opposite tactics. He should use right leg and right rein to bend the horse towards the object: the right rein controls the horse's right shoulder, and the right leg will control the quarters, while the left leg will keep the horse moving forward into the left rein, which will control the speed. The rider should not dismount and attempt to lead the horse, as he will actually have less control over him, and should he pull away and get loose on the roads, an accident may well result.

Teeth Grinding

A horse may grind his teeth together for a variety of reasons, such as being excited, annoyed, apprehensive, or merely resistant to the rider's aids. If it becomes too much of a habit, it can be very difficult to correct, other than to try and remove the cause. The bit should be checked for correct fit, and, when schooling, the rider should try to make certain that the horse is not anxious or tense (the tail can be a useful guide as to the horse's state of mind), and that he fully understands the aids, which should not be applied forcefully or roughly. If necessary, he should be prepared to take the horse back to more basic work. Often, schooling while hacking rather than in a school or *manège* is conducive to maintaining a more relaxed approach to work.

Traffic-Shyness

Riders nowadays are often forced to ride along increasingly busy roads in order to reach bridlepaths and specially constructed horsetracks. Whilst not being an ideal state of affairs, there is frequently little choice in the matter. A horse who is traffic-shy is not only a danger to himself and the rider, but to passing vehicles and pedestrians. If he has been badly frightened or injured in a road accident, he may prove impossible to hack out along roads, and he must be worked only in a safe environment away from traffic.

It may be possible to improve some horses in time by grazing them in a field alongside the road, although fencing and gates must obviously be well maintained and correctly secured in such locations. As

Fig 106 Courtesy to passing motorists is appreciated, creating goodwill and promoting consideration for other riders who may have difficult horses.

the horse becomes accustomed to, and less disturbed by, passing vehicles, the rider can progress to riding him along the perimeter of the field. When he is confident doing this, he can then be taken out along a quiet road in the company of a calm companion horse who can be ridden alongside (road visibility permitting, otherwise he should be positioned in front) so as to form a buffer between him and passing vehicles. Riding double when possible also encourages motorists to slow down when overtaking rather more than they would perhaps normally do.

The rider should be one who is able to impart quiet confidence to the horse, rather than someone who freezes and tenses up when the horse displays anxiety, which will only make him more worried. With time, it may be possible gradually to improve the horse's behaviour on the roads, but it is unlikely ever to become 100 per cent reliable and it is thus best to stick to quiet roads, and preferably in the company of another steady horse.

Whip-Shyness

There are occasions when a rider needs to reinforce the leg aids in some way, but this can be a problem if the horse is frightened of the whip. The resultant panic when it is used is undesirable and, in some cases,

Safety: Especially if it is necessary to ride out alone, the rider should inform someone at the yard of the specific route which will be taken, and the approximate time it will take. A pocket first-aid kit should be carried, and money for telephone calls.

Riding on the roads in conditions of poor visibility should be avoided altogether, even if the horse is excellent in traffic. Horses are often difficult for motorists to see clearly until it is too late in such conditions. Riders should also take the precaution of wearing fluorescent and reflective clothing: many such garments are available for both horse and rider and make them far more easily seen. Courtesy should not be forgotten: acknowledging drivers who slow down when passing horses does much to promote goodwill towards other riders. If it is not safe for the rider to remove a hand from the reins, acknowledgement can still be made by inclining the head.

Fig 107 There are many fluorescent and reflective garments available for both horse and rider. There is no excuse for not being as highly visible as possible to traffic on the roads.

the horse becomes increasingly anxious whenever he sees the whip move, even if it is not actually used. Some horses become so worried by the rider even carrying a whip that he cannot even be safely ridden with one, however careful the rider may be about handling it.

Such behaviour is usually the result of abuse with a whip in the past. If the horse is very apprehensive about the whip, it may be best to look to some other means of reinforcing the leg aids, such as spurs. If he is constantly worrying about the whip, he will certainly not be relaxed while working or in a particularly receptive frame of mind.

CHAPTER 6

Over Fences

Jumping is an activity which should be fun for both horse and rider, not something which deteriorates into a frightening, frustrating, even painful, exercise for both. Problems most frequently arise as a result of the rider's thoughtlessness or ignorance, or through over-ambitiouness, such as erecting uninviting or unsafe fences, building combinations with incorrect distances between them, or simply attempting to jump obstacles which are beyond the horse's capabilities.

Poor riding can also be far too often a cause of jumping problems, yet inevitably it is the horse who seems to end up taking the blame for the rider's shortcomings. Insufficient schooling and preparation can be to blame, but again, the fault for this should be laid at the rider's door, rather than the horse's.

Admittedly, some horses are more athletic and courageous than others, but unless there is some kind of physical problem present, all are capable of jumping to a certain extent. It is up to the rider to recognize each individual animal's limitations and not to push him beyond them.

Safety: It is especially recommended that, when jumping, the rider wears a skull cap and back protector.

It must also be remembered that it takes time, patience and knowledgeable, consistent, competent riding to produce a horse who enjoys jumping at whatever level of ability he is capable of, and these qualities are even more vital in the case of a horse who has been frightened or has lost his confidence. Also, even the best of horses can quickly be ruined with poor riding.

Bucking Between Fences

Bucking between, or on landing after, fences is not uncommon, although it can be an unnerving and unseating experience if the rider is unprepared for it. It may be caused by high spirits and exuberance, but is more frequently caused by a certain amount of discomfort in the back region. This discomfort may be the result of the rider landing heavily on the horse's back, or sitting up too early, an ill-fitting saddle, which gives inadequate clearance of the withers or pinches, or the horse feeling a twinge through his back after he has made a particularly athletic jump over a large or demanding obstacle. If the bucking is caused by the rider repeatedly landing heavily on the horse's back or an ill-fitting saddle, the horse may also be observed to jump in a rather hollow manner.

Fig 108 Crooked approaches to fences are often related to rushing problems.

Crookedness

Crooked Approaches to Fences

This is usually related to rushing *(see page 139)*: the rider attempts to restrain the horse with his hands and the horse responds by trying to move crookedly since he is not being allowed to move forwards freely. This becomes more apparent if the rider's leg aids are insufficient. This method of approach can result in the horse arriving at the fence with insufficient impulsion, or at an angle where he is forced to produce an awkward jump or run out. The rider should concentrate on achieving a more equal balance between hand and leg, and apply the same remedies as for rushing.

Crooked over Fences

A horse who drifts to one side over a fence can present problems when riding through combinations, as not only will the horse be more difficult to hold into the second or third fence, but the striding between each element will be made more awkward, and the rider may catch a leg or foot against a jump wing.

The rider should maintain a firm contact on the rein to the side on which the horse tends to drift, and apply a strong leg aid on that side, backed up by a tap on the shoulder from the stick if necessary. Approaching the fence from that side will also help a little when schooling. The horse can also be encouraged to jump straighter when working at home by either leaning a 'V' of poles against the front rail of the fence, or by suspending a single pole at an angle from the wing to the diagonally opposite corner. The rider should also check on his own straightness, as the problem will be exacerbated by a rider who continually leans to one side over the fence.

Fig 109 Using a 'V' of poles to encourage the horse to jump straight. Note that the rider has a tendency to lean to the right, which will encourage the horse to drift in that direction.

Fig 110 A single rail can be used to prevent the horse from drifting to one side.

Refusing

This is probably the most common of all jumping problems, and there are a number of reasons which may lie at the root of it:

1. Fences too high or too wide. Pushing a horse beyond his capabilities will soon frighten him, particularly if he attempts to jump and ends up hitting the fence very hard, or even becoming entangled with it.

2. Unfamiliarity. A horse may refuse certain types of obstacle that are unfamiliar to him, for example ditches, water fences, combinations, or those with an unusual and perhaps brightly painted appearance. Matters usually improve with increased experience, but initially the horse's confidence must be developed by introducing a variety of fences at small heights that are well within his scope. Horses who are naturally very wary and suspicious may benefit from being allowed to walk up to and look at the fence first before being asked to jump it.

3. Ill-fitting tack. The saddle should be a good fit, giving plenty of clearance between the front arch and the withers so that it does not catch the horse's back as he goes over the fence, especially if he tends to jump very round. Care should always be taken not to over-bit the horse; particularly if he is one who tends to get strong or excitable on his approaches it is often tempting to put something a little more severe in his mouth. While additional brakes may sometimes be a sensible course of action to pursue, it is not always the most satisfactory answer (see page 139) if the rider is less than sensitive with

his hands. A horse who feels thus over-restricted may start either to pull harder and fight the contact or, more commonly, will falter on the approach and possibly refuse.

4. Bad approach. The horse should be given the best possible line of approach: straight, rather than at an angle, with sufficient room to get to the fence. A bad stride can also be responsible for a less athletic or bold horse stopping, probably quite sensibly if it really is a difficult stride with the horse arriving either too close or too far off from the fence to jump it successfully. Using placing poles at a distance of approximately 9ft (2.5m) away from the fence can be useful in bringing the horse onto a correct take-off stride and in helping the rider to develop a better eye for a good stride so that he is able to assist the horse in the future.

5. Light. Although a horse's eyesight is generally better in poor light conditions than that of a human's, it cannot adjust to abrupt changes as rapidly, and thus problems are sometimes encountered when jumping from a well-lit area into a shady one. The horse should be steadied on his approach to such fences (although without a loss of impulsion) so as to give him as much time as possible for the eyesight to adjust. Light-coloured poles in bright sunny conditions can also sometimes cause problems as they tend to reflect light and can be difficult for the horse to judge.

6. Bad going. Ground conditions should always be taken into consideration, as these are not always ideal for jumping. A churned-up approach will not inspire great confidence in the horse, as he will

Fig 111 A poor rider position (left) can be responsible for the horse refusing. Getting left behind or catching the horse in the mouth will soon cause extreme reluctance to jump.

tend to slip as he takes off, while if the ground is very hard, he will jar his legs each time he lands, with the resultant soreness in the forelegs eventually producing a marked lack of enthusiasm for jumping.

7. Poor rider position. The rider's position may be to blame: if the horse finds that he is repeatedly jabbed in the mouth or that the rider lands with a crash on his back, he will soon start to stop. Other common positional faults include looking down at the base of the fence on the approach, too tight a rein contact, insuffi-

cient leg resulting in a lack of co-ordination and impulsion in the horse, leaning forward too soon, and dropping the rein contact just before take off, thereby abruptly unbalancing the horse.

8. Physical pain. Pain should not be ruled out as a reason for the horse refusing, and if it is felt that this could be a cause, a thorough veterinary inspection should be requested.

9. Tiredness.

10. Nappiness. The fence may be sited in

Fig 112 Here the rider has anticipated the jump, tipping forward, losing impulsion, and looking at the base of the fence, resulting in a refusal.

Fig 113 The same horse and rider a moment later, but this time the rider has used more leg to send the horse forward into the rein contact, adopting a more balanced and positive position and looking ahead rather than towards the ground.

Fig 114 Sometimes doing a bit of cross-country work or hunting will restore a horse's enthusiasm for jumping if he has become stale. (Photo: Mike Wood)

a position where the horse is required to move away from his companions or the exit of the jumping area (see page 125).

11. Staleness. Jumping the horse too frequently may make him stale and sour. The best solution is to give the horse a break completely from jumping, and then when he is reintroduced, care taken not to overdo it. Often, taking the horse hunting, or allowing him to do a few cross-country competitions will reawaken some of his old zest.

If the horse refuses more than once at the same fence, it should be reduced in size – if necessary, to the extent where the horse can just step over it – and only when both horse and rider are tackling it with confidence should it be raised again, in gradual stages. It can help considerably to have some experienced assistance on the ground to help analyse problems; often the cause is more readily discernible to an observer than to the rider.

When jumping strange obstacles, the horse's desire to remain with his companions can sometimes be used to advantage, and a lead given by another horse will often work successfully. The rider should take care not to get too close to the heels of the lead horse however, and should be prepared for a somewhat bigger jump than the size of the fence would seem to merit.

Running Out

The reasons listed under 'Refusing' (*see* pages 135–8) can also account for the

> **Safety:** Jump cups should never be left on fence wings unless a pole is resting on top of them. They can cause serious injury should the rider or horse fall against them.

horse running out at fences. The rider should be especially careful to present the horse straight at the obstacle, not at an angle, and if the horse has a tendency to run out to one particular side, the whip should be carried in that hand. The moment the rider feels the horse trying to duck out to one side, the leg on that side should be used strongly, backed up by a smack on the shoulder from the whip if necessary.

The rider should also check on his position: tipping forward too early in anticipation of the jump will allow the horse ample opportunity to run out if he wishes. Allowing the horse to escape from between hand and leg will also make it possible for the horse to evade in this manner. Too fast an approach will make matters worse, and the best solution is to reduce the size of the fence and jump it from trot, and then from an active, controlled canter. If the horse does succeed in running out to one side, the fence should be approached again from that rein.

When schooling, it is best to build fences that have substantial wings to help guide the horse into the centre of the fence. If necessary, a pole can be rested at each end of the fence, sloping down to the ground in front of it, discouraging the horse from running out. Very narrow, trappy fences should be avoided until the horse is more reliable.

Fig 115 Presenting a horse at a difficult angle to a fence can be a prime cause of his running out.

Rushing

Horses of an excitable temperament, prone to hotting up will often rush their fences, as may those who are lacking in confidence, and who try to use speed to get themselves over obstacles. Rushing is more frequently a symptom of anxiety than of enthusiasm and can be dangerous for both horse and rider, leading as it does to ill-judged take-offs, inaccurate jumping, and unbalanced landings.

Basic schooling on the flat will do much to increase the rider's control and rapport with the horse; promoting obedience, suppleness and acceptance of the aids it will give the horse a disciplined foundation on which to fall back when confronted with work of a more exciting nature. Schooling on the flat can gradually be extended to

Fig 116 A return to more basic work over poles may well be necessary in the case of the horse who rushes his fences.

encompass working over poles on the ground, and once the horse is working calmly and sensibly over these in walk and trot, a small cross-pole fence can be introduced at the end of the line of poles. Initially the horse should be encouraged to jump out of trot rather than canter, since this is less likely to excite or worry him, and the rider can exercise greater control. Eventually the rider can progress to working over small grids of fences, using placing poles where appropriate to encourage a steady approach with the horse jumping from impulsion rather than speed. Until the horse tackles small fences calmly, there is no point in raising them,

as this will only make the horse anxious and he will revert to his former behaviour. The rider should also take care not to over-ride this type of horse.

It can be a useful ploy to school the horse on the flat around a few fences, but without always jumping them, perhaps occasionally popping over one when the horse is calm and relaxed. This will help to prevent the horse from anticipating jumping whenever he is near a fence.

There may be other reasons for rushing – pain from the bit, the saddle, or the poor position of the rider – and steps should be taken to remedy these if they are the cause. Resorting to a more severe bit may

Safety: While gridwork can be extremely useful, the rider should be knowledgeable on the subject and aware of the need for correct spacing to suit each horse's length of stride and athletic ability if it is to be both beneficial and safe. If necessary, the services of an experienced instructor should be sought.

Fig 117 Eventually, the rider can progress to working over small grids of fences. (Photo: D. May)

be necessary on occasion, but is not always the answer, as it tends to encourage the rider to rely on the rein contact for control and to neglect to ride the horse forward into the bridle. The resulting lack of co-ordination and impulsion can then lead to the horse refusing or running out. Combining over-strong leg aids with an over-strong hand can also lead to problems, as the horse may begin to rush to escape the rider rather than move forward in obedience to him.

Patient, quiet schooling is really the best solution to this problem: there are no shortcuts, and the process of retraining the horse may take some time.

Refusing to Jump into Water

Water fences are becoming an increasingly popular feature of many local cross-country courses, and can provide good spectator sport since many horses are insufficiently prepared for such obstacles.

Unless the horse is evidently displaying signs of simply being stubborn, it is best to try and avoid using force, which will reinforce the horse's anxieties and make him even more reluctant to enter the water. A beach can be an ideal schooling ground, when the horse can be worked along the edge of the water when it is at low tide, and gradually ridden closer and closer until finally he is splashing through the edge. Unfortunately, not many people have access to such facilities!

An area of water needs to be found to school through – perhaps a local shallow stream, or hiring the facilities of a local cross-country course will offer the solution. It should be possible to enter it from a shallow, gradually sloping approach, as this will give the horse confidence in his footing. The bottom should be firm rather than boggy, for the same reason.

Having found some suitable water, the

Fig 118 Water fences are becoming an increasingly popular attraction at many cross-country courses, and it helps to practise over such obstacles first to prepare the horse for competition.

Fig 119 The rider should try to maintain a steady pace and impulsion when moving through water. Allowing the horse to rush can cause problems, as the drag of the water will unbalance him.

horse should be ridden towards it in walk since attempting to use speed is unlikely to result in success, but may lead to the rider getting a ducking instead! The horse should be urged on with legs and voice, and perhaps a tap from the whip if it is deemed necessary, but the latter should not be over-used. Sometimes the horse can be induced to walk into the water following the rider on foot, especially if a few favourite titbits are also offered. An often successful approach is to try and obtain some assistance from a few other riders, one to lead, one on each side and one to bring up the rear, so that the horse is sandwiched between several horses.

Once the horse has entered the water, he should be praised, and walked around in it a little until he is happy about the water splashing around his legs. The horse should be walked in and out of the water several times, and then the rider can trot through it, taking care to maintain plenty of impulsion, and not allowing the horse to rush.

When the horse is at ease with this, a pole can be placed on the edge of the water – a couple of oil drums to rest it on can be an asset – and the rider can practise jumping into, and out of, water. Care should always be taken to move steadily rather than with speed through or into water, as it will tend to drag at the horse's legs and can disrupt the balance. The rider should also remain alert when the horse is going through water, as some will try to roll in it – the first sign that this is about to happen is the horse starting to paw at it (*see* page 126).

CHAPTER 7

Travelling

If a horse has had a bad journey in the past, it is not surprising if he develops a marked reluctance to co-operate in the future. Problems encountered in connection with travelling are usually the result of such trips, especially if they have also been combined with rough, inconsiderate handling. There can also be other reasons for the horse becoming difficult, such as if he associates travelling with an event he finds unpleasant, such as a trip to a vet, or if he is only travelled when going to shows, which he may not find particularly enjoyable.

Even if the horse has never had any bad experiences of travelling – or indeed, if he has never travelled before – trailers and horseboxes are not the most inviting of vehicles to animals who are essentially wary of small, confined, dark spaces. Trailers can also feel less stable underfoot than horseboxes, while the ramps of the latter can often pose problems because of the height of the chassis, thereby making it difficult for the horse to see inside.

When the horse walks up the ramp of either, the noise made by his hooves can be alarming, and noise can be an important factor in how well he travels during a journey. Both trailers and horseboxes can assail the horse with a number of frighting noises ranging from rattling bodywork, engine whine, tyre noise, passing traffic, and the banging of ramps being raised and lowered. While some horses find this less distressing than others, journeys can be made less stressful by reducing noise to a minimum. This can be effected to a degree by adding good insulation under the floor and on walls and ceilings (without blocking ventilation ducts) and by stuffing the ears with cotton wool. A 6in (15cm) deep layer of dampened sawdust on the floor will also help muffle noise as well as providing secure footing.

Consider all this, and add to it the fact that when the vehicle is in motion the horse has to attempt to balance himself as best he can without being able to anticipate acceleration, deceleration and turns, and it is a wonder that horses will tolerate being loaded into, or travelled in, horseboxes and trailers at all!

Clothing

The horse should wear protective clothing, both when actually travelling, even for short trips, and when being taught to load and unload. Accidents can happen despite every care being taken by the handler or driver. There are various articles of clothing that should be worn.

Travelling Bandages / Leg Protectors

These should be worn to protect the legs of the horse should he lose his balance, or

Fig 120 Even on short trips, or when teaching the horse to load, protective clothing should be used on the horse.

become fractious during loading/ unloading and step off the side of the ramp. There are some very good leg protectors on the market, which also afford some protection to the coronet as well as the legs, which can be useful in preventing treads. They also have an advantage over bandages in that they are quick and easy to put on. Youngsters wearing them for the first time may panic, and so it is advisable to accustom the horse to their feel first before teaching him to load, so that he does not have to cope with too many alarming experiences all at once.

Knee Caps and Hock Boots

These will protect the knee and hock joints in the event of the horse falling to his knees, or kicking out at the rear ramp or partition. The top strap should be fitted fairly snugly, so that the boot does not slip downwards, whilst the bottom strap can be left reasonably loose so that joint flexion is not impaired. As with bandages and leg protectors, the horse should first be accustomed to wearing these garments before attempting to load him.

Tail Bandage and Tail Guard

A tail bandage will protect the tail in case the horse leans against the ramp or rear partition with his quarters. The knot of the bandage should be secured at the bottom of the dock where it cannot cause pressure on the tailbone if the horse does prop himself up in this manner. A tail

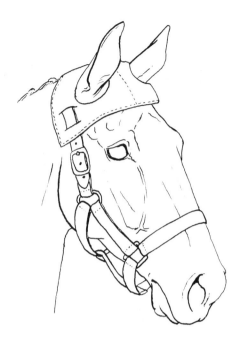

Fig 121 Poll guard. A cheap and simple alternative to a proper poll guard can be made by using a thick, broad strip of foam rubber and cutting a slit in each end for the headpiece of the headcollar to pass through.

guard, which should be attached to a roller, should be used over the top in case the bandage slips.

Poll Guard

A simple poll guard can be easily and cheaply made from a thick, oblong piece of foam rubber with a slit cut in each end through which the headpiece of the head-collar can be threaded. This will offer protection if the horse throws his head up or attempts to rear.

The handler should wear gloves to protect the palms of the hands in the event of the horse pulling away.

Barging

Barging In

This is usually associated with a lack of discipline and respect for the handler's authority generally and can be dealt with in the same manner as discussed in the sections on leading and door barging (see pages 42 and 67). It is advisable to lead the horse in a bridle, rather than a head-collar.

Fig 122 As much care should be taken unloading as loading if neither horse nor handler are to be injured or bad habits acquired. Here the handler is walking in advance of the pony, is not wearing gloves or holding the lead rope with due care, or making any attempt to keep the pony straight as he comes down the ramp. The pony is not wearing any protective boots or bandages.

Barging Out

As frustrating for the handler as a horse who refuses to set foot upon a trailer or horsebox ramp is one who walks straight into the interior, and then rapidly reverses out again. An assistant should be ready to secure the breeching strap behind the horse the moment he is inside the vehicle to prevent this happening, although care should be taken to ensure that the height of it is such that the horse cannot back out underneath it. If necessary, a yard broom can be held against the quarters by an assistant while another fastens the breeching strap in order to discourage the horse from backing out before it can be fastened.

Kicking

This may be the result of pent-up energy, or the horse feeling over-confined, or it may be because he enjoys the sound (*see* page 69). It can lead not just to damage to the vehicle, but also injury to the horse's legs and hocks. He can be given a haynet to help occupy him, and should wear hock boots to protect the joints. The interior of the vehicle can be padded to absorb both the sound and the shock of the kick.

Pawing and Scraping

This most frequently occurs when the vehi-cle is stationary, the horse being too busy maintaining his balance to do so when in motion. If there is a door-type partition in front of the horse over which he can place his head, this can result in damage to the knees, and so knee boots should be placed on the horse and the partition padded.

Refusal to Load

Before attempting to teach a horse to load, or to re-educate him, he should first be obe-dient to lead and handle generally. Plenty of time should be allowed for the proce-dure: rushing will make the horse even more anxious, and rapidly leads to frayed tempers and rough, impatient handling, with resultant bad associations for the horse, which is likely to prove troublesome in the future.

The interior of the trailer should be as inviting as possible, preferably positioned so that light shines into it, making it look less sinister. If there is a partition inside, it can be either moved to one side or removed altogether so as to give more room. In the case of trailers, an ideal model to use for difficult or novice loaders is a front-unload one. The front ramp can then be lowered so that the horse can see right through and is more likely to enter.

The trailer or horsebox should be sited on level ground so that the edge of the ramp lies flat against it and does not bounce under the horse's weight. In the case of a

---

Safety: Once the horse is on the move, he will generally stop kicking because he needs to use all four legs to help balance himself. If absolutely necessary, hobbles may be used, but these should be slack enough to allow the horse to brace himself properly against the motion of the vehicle. They should be put on after the horse has been loaded, and removed before unloading him again.

> **Safety:** If the horse is travelled with another, partitions should be provided to prevent kicking, except when travelling mares with foals at foot. The partitions should be wide enough to allow the horses to spread their legs apart sufficiently to keep their balance. If the partitions are not very high, they should be tied up short enough to prevent any aggression on the part of one horse against another.
>
> When travelling two horses together in a trailer, the heaviest should be placed on the side nearest the middle of the road (the right-hand side if driving in the UK) and if one animal is being travelled using a partition, he should also ride on the right to help counter the camber of the road.

trailer, the jockey wheel and trailer jacks should also be lowered, even if it is hitched up to a car, as it will stop the car suspension from bouncing, which can make the horse lose his balance and feel insecure. The ramp should also be covered with some kind of non-slip surface such as rubber or coconut matting; old carpeting which is often used, is not particularly ideal for the purpose since it is slippery beneath metal-shod hooves. Some form of bedding or non-slip matting should also be placed inside.

Gates that fold out to lie at either side of the ramp and form a fence on each side can be helpful in keeping the horse straight as he moves into the trailer or horsebox, preventing him from stepping off the side. If these are not present, the trailer or horsebox can be parked alongside a wall or fence, which will provide a barrier on one side. Care should be taken to site the vehicle in a safe area, away from wire fences, and it is best to load from a surface that is not slippery.

The handler should walk beside the horse so as not to obscure his vision, or place himself in danger should the horse either rear or plunge forward. He should not attempt to pull at the horse's head, as this will only provoke resistance in the opposite direction. If it looks as though the horse will pull back, attach a long lunge rein to the headcollar (or bridle if one is being used) so that he cannot break free and escape. Rather than pulling back against the horse, the handler should go with him, otherwise a tug-of-war will ensue which the horse, with his superior strength, will inevitably win and learn from. He should not be frightened or bullied in any way by the handler, but only receive pressure and encouragement from the rear should this be necessary.

Some horses may refuse to load out of stubbornness and as a challenge to the handler's authority, but it is usually best to give them the benefit of the doubt. In the case of a youngster especially, he should be allowed to stop at the bottom of the ramp and allowed to inspect the trailer. If, when he is asked to move forward, he shows reluctance, the hesitancy can often be overcome by lifting a hoof and placing it on the ramp, so that he realizes that it is quite stable and safe. Offering a scoop or bucket with some food in it may be enough to overcome the last of the horse's fears and entice him inside where he can be praised and rewarded further.

In the case of more recalcitrant animals, where gentle persuasion proves ineffective, firmer measures may be necessary, but should be carried out with the minimum of fuss, without shouting, or

Fig 123 Here, a reluctant loader is encouraged to walk up the ramp by offering a bowl of feed. Note the height of the ramp, which can sometimes cause problems if the horse suffers from back problems. Although the handler is well in advance of the horse, she is making no attempt to pull on the lead rope, which would cause the horse to pull back in resistance.

resorting to thrashing the horse about his quarters with a whip. An assistant holding the bristle end of a broom against his quarters is often surprisingly effective in inducing the horse to move up the ramp.

Another successful method is to tie a lunge rein to one side of the trailer or lorry, with an assistant holding the end so that it forms a barrier alongside the edge of the ramp. As the handler heads up the ramp, the assistant walks around the rear of the horse's quarters to the other side, shortening and tightening the lunge rein so that he is pushed in. The rein should not be flapped around as this will only frighten the horse.

This method is even more successful if two assistants are available: each holds a lunge rein tied to each side of the trailer.

Each assistant moves across behind the horse, changing sides and tightening the pressure of the lunge rein against the quarters as before, so that the horse is in effect pushed into the trailer. The assistants, as well as the handler, should wear gloves to protect the palms of the hands. Care should also be taken by the assistants to remain out of kicking distance in case the horse lashes out.

Once the horse is inside the trailer, he should be rewarded and praised lavishly, and perhaps even given a small feed before allowing him to walk out of the trailer again. The handler should encourage the horse to move straight down the ramp, especially if it is a rear-unload model where the horse has to walk out backwards; a guiding hand on the shoulder will help. The horse should also

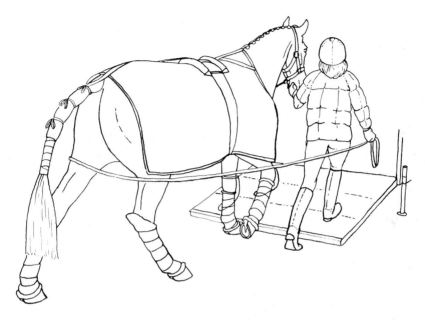

Fig 124 A method of using a lunge rein to encourage the horse to load when the handler has to cope on his own. The lunge rein is attached to one side of the lorry or trailer, passes around the horse's quarters and back to the handler by the horse's head. This method can also be used with a horse who tries to rush out backwards, although an assistant is needed to secure the breeching strap for the handler, who will be unable to reach it from inside.

be encouraged to walk out slowly, a step at a time, so that he does not slip or become unbalanced and frighten himself.

Very steep ramps can sometimes present problems, the horse having difficulty in moving up or down them, especially if he has back problems and actually experiences pain due to the gradient. This can be overcome by backing the trailer or horsebox up to a bank, or specially constructed platform on which the edge of the ramp can lie, making the gradient less steep.

Attention should also be paid to the dimensions of the interior, which must provide adequate room for the size of the animal, both to each side of him and above his head if he is not to feel trapped and dis-inclined to enter, particularly if he is slightly claustrophobic. Some horses do suffer severe claustrophobia (*see* page 65), and it may never be possible to travel such animals safely.

The horse should be loaded and unloaded again several times and, if possible, for several days afterwards before attempting a short journey. The horse should be allowed plenty of space within the vehicle, as he will need room in which to spread his legs apart in order to balance himself. Confining the horse within very narrow partitions will interfere with his balance, and should he fall over, he will be unable to regain his feet. In the case of trailers, it may be prudent to remove the central partition altogether and allow the horse all of the room, but if a spacious horsebox is available, an older, wiser horse as travelling companion can be a comforting and calming presence. The horse should be tied up so that he cannot turn around (and possibly attempt to scramble out over the top of the ramp if he is in a trailer) and given a haynet to occupy him. However, the handler should not travel in the back of a trailer with the horse as it could prove dangerous if the horse panics.

A short trip should be planned first, returning to the yard before unloading the horse again. It should, of course, go without saying that the driver should exercise the utmost possible care to give the horse the best possible ride.

Recommended Further Reading
Transporting Horses by Road (Threshold Books in association with the British Horse Society).
Larter, Chris and Tony Jackson, *Transporting Your Horse or Pony* (David & Charles).

Summary

Malice never was his aim . . .

(Jonathan Swift)

The horse is a highly specialized creature of flight and although he can fight if pressed, he prefers to run away and feels safest when in the company of others of his own kind. Although a herd animal, each horse has his own distinct personality and varies in temperament from his fellows. Some learn to identify particular situations (as well as people) and may therefore play one person up, but not another. Humans are unable not to send signals indicating confidence, authority, fear, etc., and horses are particularly receptive to these and will react according to his individual personality and temperament.

Compared to human offspring, the horse develops rapidly: within a day of his birth, he can (of necessity for survival) see, hear, suckle, urinate, defecate, vocalize, play, roll, scratch, and move at all gaits from walk to gallop. His capacity for learning is governed by his physical and mental development and although it is generally reckoned to have reached maturity between the ages of five and eight years, it may even then be lacking in the particular level of physical fitness and muscular development required to be able to cope adequately with the demands made by a rider. Training must therefore follow a steady, logical progression, as over-taxing the body or attempting to teach more in one go than the horse is mentally capable of absorbing can lead to resistances and confusion, and ultimately to vices and evasions. To be successful in handling and training horses, the handler or rider must also first obtain his confidence and trust, achieving dominance by intelligence rather than force, which breeds only distrust and further violence.

Horses have excellent and long memories, particularly for unpleasant experiences, and many problems can be related to past events. They are trained through repetition, association and reward, and it is as easy for a horse to learn bad habits as good ones. Horses vary in their willingness to work and to submit to human handling. They can also learn what is required of them and refuse to co-operate and, having discovered a successful evasion, they are quick to repeat it if it enables them to avoid carrying out a particularly disliked activity.

No horse will be mentally content if regularly asked to perform work for which he is not mentally or physically suited, or if he is continually over-taxed. Consideration must also be given not just to the horse's workload but also to his surroundings: a horse who is happy and relaxed in his environment and routine, with sufficient freedom out at grass permitted each day for social interaction and play, will be a far more willing and cooperative servant.

It takes time to build a good relationship (or to overcome problems) but if a particular course of action does not produce the desired results after it has been given a fair period of time, the handler or trainer must be prepared to be open minded and flexible in his way of thinking and perhaps try a different approach, which may prove more successful. It often pays to seek the advice and tuition of a good, experienced instructor if real problems are encountered as, so often, a fresh eye can throw a new light on the matter. Some problems are simply not safe for an inexperienced or novice handler or rider to deal with anyway, and are best placed in the hands of a more expert person.

Sometimes a handler and horse combination are simply temperamentally unsuited to each other, which can be the cause of much stress and unnecessary conflict on both sides. The handler must be ready to recognize such a situation and to admit defeat and sell the horse to a more suitable person, and seek something better matched to himself.

Appendix I

Methods of Restraint

There are occasions when it is necessary to restrain the horse in some manner, either to carry out everyday tasks such as grooming or mucking out, or perhaps to allow shoeing, veterinary inspection or treatment.

Horses who are difficult to handle may be so because of pain or genuine fear (perhaps as a result of a bad experience in the past) as well as out of sheer bloody-mindedness or stubbornness because he has not learnt to respect the authority of the handler. Each case needs to be treated on its own merits: with a nervous horse, it may be best to persevere in a quiet manner, reassuring him with both voice and touch to try and overcome his anxieties; a firmer approach may be needed with a bolshy horse. The handler needs to be familiar enough with a variety of horses to try and decide upon the most appropriate tactics.

Where the horse's actions make him dangerous to both himself and the people around him, human safety must, of course, be the main priority. Whenever possible though, sheer brute force should be avoided, and another method perhaps considered instead, which will probably be ultimately more successful. Once a battle of strength has been embarked upon, it is more likely to be the horse who emerges as the eventual victor, and he will have learnt that he can challenge the handler's authority and get away with it. Just as importantly, both horse and handler are likely to run the risk of injury to either party, and for young horses or those of a nervous disposition the experience will be extremely frightening, creating distrust and an ingrained habit of resistance.

Mild restraint should be used initially, only resorting to firmer measures if the situation really merits it, and the method used will be dictated by the handler's knowledge of the horse's temperament and level of education. It is particularly worth remembering that many horses, on feeling that they are powerless to move freely, will panic and fight to escape from the restraint; the instinct to flee or fight moves to the fore, often overwhelming their training.

Headcollar and Bridle

Some horses can be fractious when being led or held in a headcollar and lead rope, in which case a bridle will afford more control. Placing a headcollar lead rope through the mouth is best avoided unless there is no alternative, as it can easily cut the mucous membranes of the gums. It is far better, if a bridle is not available, to pass the lead rope over the front of the nose and back through the headcollar ring on the near side, exerting a restraining

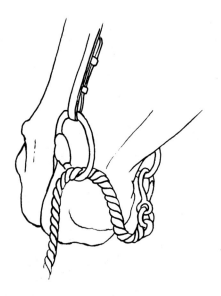

Fig 125 If a lead rope is used on a bridle, it should be clipped to the offside bit ring and passed through the nearside bit-ring.

pressure on the front of the horse's nasal bone.

When a lead rope is used on a bridle instead of reins, a leather coupling which passes beneath the jaw and clips to the bit rings on each side should be used, to which the lead rope is then attached. Alternatively, the lead rope should be clipped to the offside bit ring and then passed beneath the jaw and through the nearside bit ring. It should never be clipped to just one bit ring, since, if the horse becomes difficult, the bit may be pulled right through the mouth.

There are a few varieties of 'controller' halters on the market, which do give a greater degree of control than a conventional headcollar but with a varying amount of success on different animals.

Holding a Foreleg

A commonly used method of restraining a horse is to hold up a foreleg, which will force him to stay still in order to balance on the other three legs, although it will not stop him from attempting to rear or throw himself down. This will also discourage him from kicking out with a hind leg while the handler is doing something which he finds ticklish (such as clipping or grooming beneath the belly) or painful (such as treating an injury). One person will be needed to hold the horse's leg up, while another holds the head and reassures the horse if necessary. If the handler is working on the left side of the horse, the left foreleg should be held up so as to

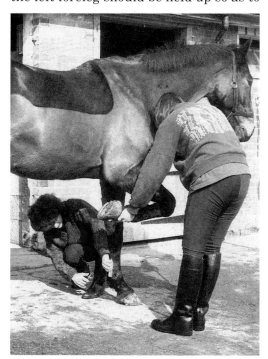

Fig 126 Holding up a foreleg to prevent the horse from fidgeting while being trimmed up.

make it more difficult for the left hind leg to strike out and vice versa.

Alternatively, should the handler wish to carry out some task involving the forelegs, treating for injury, or trimming up, for example, and the horse is being fidgety and unco-operative, the assistant should lift up the opposite foreleg to help keep the one being worked on, firmly on the ground. This will also apply to the hind legs.

Pinching a Fold of Skin

A simple method of restraint is to pinch a fold of the loose skin at the base of the neck just in front of the shoulders. It is thought that this may be an acupuncture point, as with twitching (*see below*).

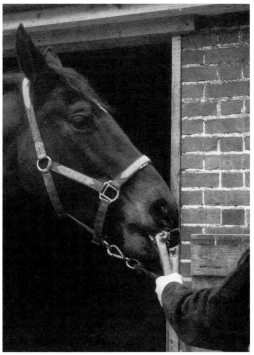

Fig 128 Twitch.

Twitch

The twitch consists of a length of smooth wood with a hole in one end through which a loop of rope or plaited twine has been passed. The handler places one hand through the loop of the twitch and then grasps the horse's upper lip firmly with the fingers. The loop is then passed over the hand and around the lip and the twitch handle twisted so as to tighten the loop. Since most horses do not relish this procedure, an assistant will be needed to help hold the horse while the twitch is being fitted. The edges of the lip should be folded downwards so that the loop of rope does not cut the inner linings.

Occasionally the handler may come across a horse who fights the twitch, and

Fig 127 Pinching a fold of loose skin at the base of the neck.

such horses are probably more dangerous with it on than off. On the whole, though, it tends to be a largely effective method of restraint for procedures which the horse strongly objects to, or when it is essential that it stands very still.

Once the twitch is in place, give it a moment or two to take effect before commencing with whatever the task is: the horse will stand stock still, and the eyes will appear slightly glazed. It is thought that the reason for such a reaction is not intense pain (although it cannot be an entirely comfortable experience) but that the area may possibly be an acupuncture point. Pressure applied to the area causes the release of endorphins within the body (endorphins are painkillers far more effective than morphine), and the horse in effect sedates himself.

The effectiveness of twitching varies in duration, and should not be left on for more than fifteen minutes, after which period the horse may begin to show signs of restlessness. If the task has not been completed, the horse can be left for a short while and then the twitch replaced. Once it has been removed, the nose should be massaged to restore circulation.

Humane twitches are available, resembling a pincer-like implement which is clamped onto the top lip, reducing the danger of cutting the skin.

Casting

Casting is an old method of restraint which is less frequently used nowadays since the development of effective tranquillizers and local and general anaesthetics. Throwing the horse to the ground in this manner does carry a risk, as he may panic as he feels his legs being pulled from underneath him. Either hobbles are used on three or four of the legs, which are then drawn together unbalancing the horse and toppling him to the ground, or a system of ropes are used which force the horse into a sitting position before he is cast onto his side. This is very much an exercise which should be left strictly to a veterinary surgeon or an experienced and knowledgeable person, and should not be attempted by anyone else.

Hobbles

Hobbles may be advocated for a horse who is difficult to catch, as they will restrict the pace at which he can move. They should not be used on horses who are turned out with company, however, as he will be unable to defend himself if he is bullied.

The bracelets passing around the fetlocks (generally on the front legs) must be well padded to prevent chafing, and it should be remembered that this form of restraint can carry risks for the horse. He should be accustomed to them by degrees, first being led carefully round the stable wearing them, then the yard and finally the field, so he has a chance to get used to the restriction of stride. It is best to avoid using them on nervy animals altogether, since should he panic, he is very likely to bring himself down and be unable to rise again, frightening and possibly injuring himself in the process.

Tethering

A method sometimes used to restrict the movements of hard-to-catch horses, or of utilizing unfenced common land for grazing, is tethering. This can present certain problems, most notably the lack of available shelter and water supply, and some horses actually manage to free themselves and wander off. Horses not accustomed to being tethered must be accustomed to it gradually, and initially, at least, must be closely supervised in case they become entangled in the tether and panic, possibly bringing themselves down and probably incurring rope burns.

The stake used to attach the tether to should be hammered deeply and firmly into the ground so that it cannot be easily pulled up by the horse, and tether ropes or chains with swivels used. The horse will need to be moved regularly, since his grazing area will obviously be somewhat limited. Either a closely fitting stout headcollar or a stout, padded neck collar may be used to attach the tether to the horse; a neck collar is probably less likely to be slipped off or to chafe.

Sedatives

The use of sedatives and tranquillizers can in some instances make certain operations safer for both horse and handler, and a vet should be consulted if chemical restraint of some kind is necessary.

Tranquillizers and sedatives are administered by injection or by mouth, their effect varying from mild tranquillization to profound sedation. Incorrectly administered, or given in the wrong dosage, some drugs can have a detrimental effect on blood pressure and the central nervous system, and so should only be given by either a veterinary surgeon, or the handler under strict veterinary supervision.

Signs that the drug is taking effect will include a drooping of the head and lower lip hanging loosely, and a glazed look in the eyes. While some drugs result in the horse standing stock still, others may leave the horse with a slight degree of unsteadiness on his feet. He should be sedated in the area where whatever task is to be undertaken will be carried out; the handler should not attempt to move an animal under sedation as his movements will be unco-ordinated and he may stumble and injure himself. This is not a particularly ideal form of restraint for use on animals who are difficult to shoe for exactly this reason; when being shod the horse needs to be in full control of his balance in order to stand on three legs.

Depending upon the drug used, the dosage administered, and the temperament of the horse, the time during which the sedation will last can vary greatly. Sometimes the horse can be more amenable to certain operations, such as clipping, after having been sedated the first time. Although not fully aware of surroundings as normal, he is not completely knocked out and it is sometimes the case that having had no choice but to submit to the procedure, and having discovered that he has not been hurt, he will gain in confidence and trust, and be more co-operative the next time.

Keeping a Horse Down

There may be occasions when it is necessary to restrain a horse who is lying down from attempting to stand up, in order to prevent him from struggling further and possibly injuring himself: for example, if the horse has colic and is attempting to roll violently, or if he has become cast and is panicking. The easiest way to keep him temporarily still is to place one knee on the neck just behind the cheekbone. If the horse is unable to raise his head, he cannot lift his front end up, and so is forced to remain lying down.

Appendix II

The Equine Behaviour Study Circle

The Equine Behaviour Study Circle (EBSC) is an international group of enthusiasts from all walks of life who are interested in how horses behave and why they do the things they do. Members comprise professional and amateur horse people, veterinary surgeons, research scientists, 'weekend riders', breeders and, indeed, many people who not only do not have their own horses, ponies, mules or donkeys but who never even associate with other people's – they simply like to observe them from afar or read about them.

The Circle issues a six-monthly journal, *Equine Behaviour,* which is made up almost entirely of members' observations on equine behaviour, both normal and abnormal. Many members have found the information in the journal, and the observations and ideas of other members, of particular help in sorting out problems in their own animals.

The Circle organizes visits for members and guests to places of interest in the horse world and encourages them to attend its informal and always friendly talks and discussions.

Full details about the EBSC can be obtained by writing to the treasurer, Mrs Jane Lucas, Flat 2, 169 Sumatra Road, West Hampstead, London NW6 1PE, England. The Circle's North American co-ordinator is Dr Sharon E. Cregier, University of Prince Edward Island, Charlottetown, Prince Edward Island, Canada C1A 4P3. The Australasian co-ordinator is Mrs Sheree Cavaye, Lot 12, Singleton Road, Wilberforce, NSW 2756, Australia.

Index